Transparent Teaching of Adolescents

Defining the Ideal Class for Students and Teachers

Mindy Keller
Written in conversation with
Stacey Bruton
AnnMarie Dearman
Victoria Grant
Crystal Jovae Mazur
Daniel Powell
Christina Salvatore

ROWMAN & LITTLEFIELD EDUCATION

A division of
ROWMAN & LITTLEFIELD PUBLISHERS, INC.
Lanham • New York • Toronto • Plymouth, UK

Published by Rowman & Littlefield Education
A division of Rowman & Littlefield Publishers, Inc.
A wholly owned subsidiary of The Rowman & Littlefield Publishing Group, Inc.
4501 Forbes Boulevard, Suite 200, Lanham, Maryland 20706
www.rowman.com

10 Thornbury Road, Plymouth PL6 7PP, United Kingdom

British Library Cataloguing in Publication Information Available

Library of Congress Cataloging-in-Publication Data
Keller, Mindy, 1966- author.
  Transparent teaching of adolescents : defining the ideal class for students and teachers / Mindy Keller.
      pages cm
  Includes bibliographical references and index.
  ISBN 978-1-61048-914-0 (cloth : alk. paper) — ISBN 978-1-61048-915-7 (pbk. : alk. paper) — ISBN 978-1-61048-916-4 (electronic) (print)
  1. High school teaching. 2. Classroom management. I. Title.
  LB1737.A3K45 2012
  373.1102—dc23
                                                                    2012018808

♾TM The paper used in this publication meets the minimum requirements of American National Standard for Information Sciences—Permanence of Paper for Printed Library Materials, ANSI/NISO Z39.48-1992.

Printed in the United States of America

To all of the students who had a part in
creating this teacher and our classes

Contents

List of Figures

Preface

I once commented to a class, "You know, if I had enough money around to cover bills and stuff, I would teach for free. I love working with you guys."

Their response was to shake their heads and roll their eyes at what they saw as my usual insanity—a teacher who loves her job enough to do it without getting paid.

"Yeah, right. You on drugs, Ms. K?" they ventured.

Why was I so dippity-doo in love with teaching high school and so many of my colleagues were not?

I seemed to have ideal classes.

My experiences were drastically different from my peers' daily torments and stress over behavior problems. I enjoyed my interactions with students. I looked forward to my classes. I didn't perceive teaching as *work* but as a daily opportunity to collaborate on a given challenge.

And it wasn't just one class out of seven classes. *Every class*, no matter the level or course, was an ideal class. And it wasn't just one year out of many years, but *every year* was an ideal year. Using the same kind of student-driven classroom management, feedback, and input made the difference.

These classes discussed, analyzed, created, and cooperated—they learned the subjects, but more importantly, the students seemed to *care*. Whether it was a discussion of a reading passage, a production analysis, or a research paper, they cared about *what* they were learning, *how* they were learning it, and *why*. I loved our classes.

This doesn't mean that students didn't complain (they did!). It also doesn't mean they were all perky little academics (they weren't!). However, they did exhibit the most crucial component for the ideal class—the *willingness* to learn—and that was largely due to their acceptance and embrace of the transparent teaching style.

Together, we created our classes. Together, we learned, taught, and collaborated.

My former students and fellow authors became quite intrigued with the idea of sharing the foundation of what they experienced. After all, were they not also authors of their ideal classes? Their input is as crucial to this book as it was to the class. When I initially told them about the project, Daniel replied:

> *I watched our current educational system destroy many promising teachers. If any of those teachers can be taught to find a way to bloom as you did, even in those dark corners, then I'd say your book would be a success.*

As we moved more deeply into the conversation of the class experience, we uncovered how everything fits together to create the whole. Even now, our conversation continues, but with a focus on the tangibles of how any teacher might replicate this experience.

You'll see strategies, reflections, timelines, and outlines, all of which are critically annotated by the students who experienced it. This is our conversation about what we did, what worked, what didn't, and why—a model of what occurred in our ideal classes.

Acknowledgments

I'd like to thank these individuals for their assistance and support of this project:
My husband, Costas Kyriakides
Mrs. Debbie Scherer, for asking
Miriam Diamond, for shoving me into the road
Bertram Linder, agent extraordinaire, for taking a chance
Dr. Kathy Huie, advisor, mentor, and voice
Doris McManus, for taking a chance with a student teacher
Kristen Taylor, teacher and inspiration
Tekisha Roberts, former student
Masac Dorlouis, former student
Reverend Jack McCulley, former student
Zach Russakis, former student
Linda Allen, former student
Veronica Cronin, for inspiring me
Shawn Fahy, for your moral support
Anonymous contributors

Chapter One

Understanding and
Visualizing the Ideal Class

The positive outcomes were shown in your students' thoughts of you—their relationship with you. You had, and still have, a great relationship with your students because of your methodology. There's something to be said for that. I would never have opened up, come out of my shell, or become who I am today, had I not been in your classes. ~ Christina

Before you can start working towards creating the ideal class, you have to be able to visualize it for yourself. As with any project, *seeing* the goal is a large part of the plan. All of the steps that follow will point back to that visualized goal.

Consider this your time to fantasize about what you really want from yourself, your students, and the experience, all of the things that constitute what we call a "class." Do what you can to make this picture tangible. With it, you can begin to build the foundation of your ideal class.

Don't think you can do this in one sitting, either. Let it marinate for a day or two. Ask other people. Watch inspiring films. Do whatever it takes to move yourself to a point where you are able to see this class in your mind.

If you're a new teacher, a good reference point is your own experience in high school. What classes seemed "ideal" to you? What made them ideal? What did the teacher do and say? What was the work like? How did the students communicate and work together?

Veteran teachers have probably experienced shimmers of an ideal class throughout their courses. Remember that one particular assignment where all of the students seemed engaged, or that one group of students in period two who just seemed to "mesh"? No one was pandering for a hall pass or sleeping; kids were learning, and *you* were having a good time!

Now, take that glimpse and expand on it. Visualize it as the norm. How do the students approach the material and coursework in your ideal class? What do you see? What do you hear? What do you say? What do they say? How do you look and feel?

Veteran high school teacher, Kristen Taylor, describes her ideal class as:

> Strangely enough, absolutely crammed full of kids. They are an extremely diverse group—all colors, all ethnic groups. They like each other, the subject, and me. There are quiet kids, chatty kids, but everyone is absolutely comfortable speaking his or her own mind. The feeling is one of mutual respect, with the kids treating each other well. A ton is accomplished every day, and we all leave with a sense that we have done all that we can.

A beautiful image, isn't it? What's imperative about realizing this vision is that it underscores the decisions you make during teaching. It's the unspoken expectation that, when the class moves against the vision, you express surprise and concern. It's your motivation to take action and move it back.

You can get there. You can have students who are willing learners and critical thinkers, accomplishing tons each day. You can have students who are respectful to each other and you. Every class, every year. Dream big. The clearer the picture is in your mind, the closer you are.

Some students shared what they felt about this type of class:

- *You always inspired us and, most importantly, made us feel comfortable with who we were.*
- *I'm gainfully employed in the arts, and I still thank you for that. People always want to know the hows/whys. I always come back to your support—in and out of the classroom. I miss you. I miss those heated conversations in class. You were what kept me at that school.*
- *You really opened my eyes to a lot of new things in my junior year!*
- *You were my inspiration!!*
- *Thank you so much for the teaching and inspiration you've given me.*
- *You are the teacher that I consider to be probably the most influential in my youth . . . that was a very important time of my life, and I have you to thank for that.*
- *I am inspired and eternally grateful for the experience of being taught and, more importantly, cared for by you.*

These words reflect why teachers do what they do, year after year—to make that impact, to turn on that light. However, we need to acknowledge that students are the co-creators of their classroom experience. They may see us as their inspiration, but we are not the be-all and end-all of their class experience. It is our job to give them an opportunity to explore, learn, and *think* in a comfortable environment. It is our job to be *transparent*.

Chapter Two

Who Are You, Anyway?

Being involved in a community of other social orphans and helping to develop a new, safe environment within the walls of a high school is not always afforded to every student. In our class, there was never a choice to not be accepted or not be valued: we just were. I'm not sure if Ms. K made a conscience effort to teach us our worth or if it came naturally. ~ Tekisha Roberts

You've hopefully arrived at a semblance of how you see your ideal class, so now it's time to dig into the you as teacher. Let's say that there are two "yous": a teacher-you and a just-you. These two entities, though separate, should complement each other. Just-you is the person your friends and family see, or who you are when no one else is around.

Courses and prep programs rarely address the teacher-you. They'll provide you with ideas for philosophy, curriculum, and classroom management, but they don't really discuss the necessity of presenting an authentic teacher persona or how to do it.

Ironically, it's the most important component of the craft because your teacher persona is the first thing students see and evaluate. That sense of you is the most lasting, endurable memory your students will have, so this component—your teacher persona—merits some thought.

As the adage goes, we can't change anyone but ourselves. Most counseling books provide this advice, and it's valid for teaching, too. We only have control over our own actions and reactions, thoughts and words, choices and decisions. Nothing else. We do not have control over what our students choose to do or not do, say or not say. Accepting that will help you move towards a solid teaching persona.

For a moment, don't think about how awful teenagers can be or how inconsiderate administration can be or the overwhelming performance pressure placed on you. Put those aside for a bit, we'll get to them.

For now, think about who you are in the classroom. Ask yourself these questions:

Do I convey a thoughtful person?
Do I convey a respectful person?
Do I convey enthusiasm for my lessons, course, and subject?
Do I convey warmth, maturity, and acceptance?
Do I strive to make my voice pleasant?
Do I dress with care?
Do I convey that I care about myself?
Do I convey that I care for others?
Do I convey that I'm willing to learn?
Do I convey excitement about my own learning and others' learning?

Notice the focus of convey. Eventually, the goal is to become what you convey, but for now, working on conveying these things is your starting point.

Today's students are witness to some very emotionally immature and unhappy—nay, miserable!—adults. These adults may be their parents, other teachers, or even the media's portrayal of adults on shows aimed at preteens and adolescents. They see adults complaining, arguing, drinking themselves into a stupor, behaving foolishly, killing each other or their children, or self-medicating in any number of ways, too stressed out to do much more than watch television.

How many teenagers have authentically interacted with a truly mature and happy adult? If they do see one, they don't really believe it, particularly if this person is a teacher. How many times have we presented a happy, confident, mature persona at the beginning of the school year, only to have it shredded like lettuce by the end of September?

And adolescents are such a tough audience! High schoolers only know what they perceive to be "true" or "real."

The ideal classroom serves to shift that thinking into what can be. Part of that ideal classroom is composed of teachers who convey the best facets of mature adults:

• content, or proactively working to change the root of discontent
• fulfilled by their careers, or actively seeking to address needs
• excited by what they're doing, or actively seeking renewal
• knowledgeable in what can be done and interested in what might be done

- accepting of their own faults/weaknesses and motivated to change them
- interested in what others think and what others' experiences have been
- willing to be flexible
- aware of others' emotions
- readily able to acknowledge mistakes to others
- focused on the greater good
- humble, articulate, warm
- in possession of a sense of humor in general and with themselves
- willing to work with all levels of students
- adaptable to different cultural beliefs/ideals
- *aware that we're all on this earth learning together, and that although the teacher is deemed the expert of the subject, students can bring valid points to the table ~ Christina*
- *genuinely honest*

Honesty is the strongest factor for building trust. If anything ever even seems false, then the persona you build for your students is sundered. If there is one thing that defines the student/teacher bond more than any other, it's trust. So, be genuine. Be honest. ~ Daniel

This is an extensive list, and you may be thinking, "Yeah, right. This is about impossible. I can do this for about five minutes before those kids start pushing my buttons, and then I lose it."

Others might say, "I don't get it. I can't do all that. It's like you're a robot or something."

Far from it! Eventually, we'll yell, we'll cry, or we'll walk out of the room in a huff. We'll all do the wrong thing at least once, if not more. And, your students will *never* let you forget it.

You lost your temper with us on several occasions, and I believe a stress ball was completely destroyed. I learned to duck when you threw scripts, though! ~ Daniel.

The good news is—it's okay to lose it once in a while. It's okay to go off track. Really! What's *not* okay is staying off track. What's *not* okay is not owning up to your tantrums and feelings.

Students don't need us to be perfect. They need to see mature adults working through what is *not* perfect.

They need to see how to handle things when things don't go right. If we go *off* track, but immediately verbalize awareness of that lapse or error to move back *on* track, we have taught high schoolers the most valuable lesson of all: how to be an *adult*.

CONFIDENT HUMILITY AND SELF-ACCEPTANCE

This component can be tricky for some teachers. Of course, we're confident! We know our stuff! We accept ourselves without much ado. We are educated professionals, organized and creative, following procedures and policies with crisp accuracy. We know what the students need to learn and when they should learn it.

But do we convey that confidence in a way that builds rapport and trust? Are we allowing the rip tide of performance-based testing to drown our confidence? Is our self-acceptance genuine *enough* to withstand anything thrown up against it?

Consider this scenario. The teacher is lecturing on something about something, and going on and on about the Georgian calendar. She writes it on the overhead—GEORGIAN calendar. The class, diligently taking notes, copies it. She makes a joke about how Pope George's nickname was Georgie to his friends. This goes on until one student pipes up, "I think you mean *Gregorian* calendar."

(D'oh!)

This kid even has the grace to add, "I might be wrong, but I think that's what it's called."

(Double D'oh!)

Here is where the importance of humility and self-acceptance comes into play. Ms. Teacher has several options: (1) lie importantly and say, "Of course it's Georgian!"; (2) not admit the mistake at all, and just keep going; (3) dismiss the mistake casually with, "Yes, or something like that"; or (4) use this moment to teach what learning and, ultimately, being an adult is all about.

The choice of the latter, sprinkled with much laughter, sends the strongest message: "I feel really stupid, but I'm comfortable with my mistake, with me."

The teacher exclaims, "Wow! I don't think I could be more wrong! Thanks! You are absolutely right! Everybody, we need to correct this. I don't know what I was thinking just then! See what happens when you get old? Tsk."

Correcting a teacher that I respected left me with a sense of what I can only loosely describe as academic camaraderie. Camaraderie in a sense that two people can laugh at an inside joke. Had I never chuckled and bothered to voice my mind, we wouldn't have had that conversation en forum with my peers, and all of us as a momentary community. The teacher and I, and my class, would've been much poorer for it.

Surely, it is the human element of teaching that is the most important, always. For as parents pass on traits to us, what teachers share is every bit as essential to the humans that we become. ~ Rev. Jack McCulley

It is okay to make a mistake; it is not okay to be a pedantic jerk about it when you do. Being comfortable enough with yourself to acknowledge and correct mistakes, as well as being able to admit, "I don't know, but I'll look it up!" will make a difference in how students receive you. It will *permit* them to receive you, and to learn, they must be receiving. We don't necessarily start out this way, though, do we?

> *I recall the first time I met you. You were the new student teacher, starting things off abruptly and seeming very concerned with taking control immediately. You spoke in short, cut-off sentences, accentuated with breaths at the end. I got the feeling we made you nervous, but you used that nervousness to be firm.*
>
> *I wasn't sure I would be comfortable in your classroom because very stern and by-the-rules-no-leeway teachers terrified me. As the weeks went on, you became more visibly comfortable. It seemed that you were constantly trying to prove yourself worthy. I didn't feel that there was a connection between you and the class, nor with the material to teach. ~ AnnMarie*

Holy bad first impressions! This was the very first day and the very first lecture ever given to this class. It was a conglomeration of an introduction of the new student teacher as the teacher and the start of a unit in English literature—the Anglo-Saxon era. No connection to the material? Really? Pshaw! I knew my stuff! I knew I had to come across as the authority.

Weeks of preparation, awesome overhead images, historically accurate notes—*failed*, and certainly, the establishment of the class as any sort of learning community—*failed*. This is what AnnMarie remembers: someone very uncomfortable with *herself*. More importantly though, it lends an insight into how to begin a course.

We don't need confidence in *teaching* to begin the classes. We need to be comfortable with who we are. Of course, we know the content. That's what we went to college for. *What* we're going to teach has less impact than how comfortable we are in our own skins.

If we are even slightly comfortable with ourselves, we won't feel the need to prove ourselves worthy, thus losing a potential for connection and rapport with students. We will be comfortable enough to express our concerns about the class and our newness to the career. We will be comfortable and transparent enough to say: "You know, I'm new at this, so I'm going to ask you at the end of my overview how I did. I want to make sure you got the information you need, but I also want to make sure I've given it to you the best way I can."

By doing so, we won't throw up this immediate wall between ourselves and the students: we'll open a window.

> *Right! I took drama the following school year with you as my teacher, so I had an interesting basis for comparison. You again began the class as a stern, firm, these-are-the-rules teacher, but you seemed more comfortable in your role.*

You began to establish relationships with us, and I felt more comfortable coming out of my shell as well. You encouraged participation in class. Well, at first, it seemed you demanded it—which of course, terrified me—but as time wore on, it felt more like it was encouraged. ~ AnnMarie

Again, the aspect of comfort in the teacher persona seemed to prevail. That comfort AnnMarie recognized really refers to *self-acceptance*. However, that sense of comfort didn't seem to move over into discipline because she still saw an overly stern teacher, it seems. The encouragement she refers to would have (and eventually did) come from the base of self-acceptance.

I was also a witness to those first years in which a teacher grows from initial naiveté into the person he or she will become for many years afterwards. You weren't the only teacher I'd witnessed in such a state, but you were rare in that you retained your passion for your craft.

Such perseverance alone would be enough to elevate you to being one of the exceptional teachers I'd encountered, but there was something else. There was a quality to you that was different—a quality that may be replicated for other aspiring teachers: you were also a student. ~ Daniel

This replicable quality involves, then, not only the transparency of who we are as teachers, but who we are as learners.

The Transparent Learner

You learned from us. You made us feel like our input mattered. As you taught us the varied points of technical theatre and acting, you also thrived on our myriad perspectives. Due to this simple characteristic, you managed to reach me more than any other teacher had. Because while other exceptional teachers may have managed to draw out our interest as students, they were the teacher and we, the students. Not "their" students, merely "the" students.

But with you, we were all in it together. We thrived and grew off of each other. And while you were clearly the authority, the source of our knowledge, our teacher, you were also our mentor. There with us. Growing with us. ~ Daniel

It seems counterproductive, though, doesn't it? How can we teach anything if we're learning? Yet the teacher who is a willing, humble student shapes a sense of community into the classroom that wouldn't otherwise exist. Your transparency as a first-year teacher, or even more importantly as a veteran teacher, will make the difference.

In the following year, where you seemed much more confident and comfortable, I was able to see the teacher and the student. You sometimes gave anecdotes about your years in school, techniques you'd learned, or methods your instruc-

tors used. Sometimes you even compared those tidbits to activities we were working on, and occasionally you would discount those ideas.

I gradually came to realize that we were actively engaged in a dialogue with you. This included learning facilitated by you, as well as learning WITH you. I think this knowledge that you were learning, too, and that we all learn new things all the time, really allowed us to open up to you and take risks in the classroom. Teacher as learner taught me a great deal. ~ AnnMarie

Engaged in a dialogue! What an excellent way to describe our ideal class experience! Our classes did seem to be one long conversation. You'll see a bit later that this dialogue and conversation can be facilitated through thematic teaching, but it is very interesting that this dialogue is what AnnMarie remembers from the class.

When teachers become more comfortable, they can begin to function transparently as learners. The students follow by participating more willingly and more in-depth. The interest will be tangible, a roomful of students learning and thinking and obvious positive outcomes: more questions, better questions, on-task behavior. There will also be a sense of awareness and understanding of that tingly "this is how it feels to learn" in the air.

There was the understanding that you held yourself to the same standards as your students. This isn't to say you lowered yourself. You challenged us in ways other teachers didn't think to challenge us. You gave students a voice, and I put my trust in you. I am a better student, artist, and future educator for it. ~ Crystal

Again, the sense of humility comes into play: holding one's self to the same standards. While we may argue that, of course, we hold ourselves to high expectations, the difference is the explicit conveyance of it *to* and *with* students. We can expect X from them, but they can also expect X from us.

I agree, 100 percent! You asked me my opinion on things and made me feel as if I had something worthy to teach you. I developed more as a person in your class because you treated me as an adult—other teachers saw me as a "student" and an underling, nonetheless. ~ Christina

Everyone has something worthy to teach us! Some of the most profound things to be learned come from children, not adults, and humility definitely plays a role in that.

You didn't simply impart your knowledge to us, you shared it. And as you taught us, we supported you. This is the fundamental difference between your teaching methods and those of many others, the results of which are evident even in this ambitious work of yours. For even after all these years, your passion continues to guide us, and we continue to support you. ~ Daniel

This methodology that Daniel notes eventually becomes a way of *being* in the classroom. To begin your journey to transparent learner, you'll want to ask yourself these questions:

Am I open to new ideas? How can I more emphatically convey that?
Am I willing to hold myself accountable to student expectations? How can I show/demonstrate that I am?
Am I willing to allow others to explore their ideas openly? How can I authentically convey that willingness?
Am I willing to suppose and wonder explicitly, for the purposes of modelling thinking and learning? How can I convey that more consistently?

Honestly reflecting on these questions will help you begin to make the shift to transparency. Moreover, finding your teacher-you and tapping back into your origins of intellectual curiosity and humility of *not* knowing everything will open the windows in your class's experience. Windows for you and your students, no matter *where* you teach.

Students are a projection of a teacher's own self, and the teacher is the most significant student of all. ~ *International student*

In the chapters that follow, we'll address how to convey transparency in teaching through each step of creating the class. First, let's talk about how you might be conveying something completely different!

Chapter Three

How You Convey Persona

THE VOICE

I had so many teachers in high school that had no inflection whatsoever in their voices, which led me to be completely disinterested in the subject matter, despite how compelling that subject may have been. ~ Christina

As teachers, our voice is our most powerful tool. How we use this instrument, with what tone, resonance, pitch, articulation, and projection, profoundly impacts students' learning and learning *experiences*. However, the use of voice is another component that may not be addressed in educational coursework or evaluations. It may be assessed or evaluated as a component of an academic presentation, perhaps, but the use of voice as an instrument of conveyance merits more detailed analysis.

The voice is the primary means by which we convey our teacher persona, and that tool needs continual honing and polishing. It must not be allowed to go dull.

Before giving a mini-lecture or presentation, explain to students that if they hear your voice going nasal, monotone, or weird sounding, they are to let you know. This transparent evaluative instruction ensures that (1) you don't bore them to death or (2) distract them from *what* you have to say.

Everyone's voice sometimes drifts off into something (even movie stars' voices), and we lose nothing by reminding students that we are aware of this phenomenon.

For example, who wants to listen to someone who sounds like she's sucked the helium out of a dozen balloons? Who's going to take that voice seriously? Note that by addressing the awareness of shortcomings, this transparent humility begins to connect the students to the teacher.

A large part of teaching is performing. A good teacher absolutely needs to get the students interested and engaged. Excitement for the subject thrown in every now and again is helpful because a monotone lecture is the worst!

I had a teacher, who was a wonderful man, but when he stood at the front of the room and gave a lecture (while we copied notes from the overhead projector) the words tended to blur together, particularly because he didn't vary his tone or pitch or volume. I believe he was genuinely excited about a topic twice, because his voice changed, and the whole class stopped to look at him. Fortunately, he had a nice voice. Unfortunately, it always made me so comfortable that I felt I could sleep right then and there.

On the other hand, I also had a teacher who couldn't keep the same tone or pitch or volume to save her life. The constant up-and-down threw my brain in the fryer. Variety is good, but it should not be constant. It should be enough to get attention, but not so much that students want to cover their ears. Speaking of covering my ears—I also had a teacher with a very nasal voice. The first day in class, I had to keep looking closely to make sure she wasn't pinching her nose or wearing a nose clip. It was unnerving. I would like to say I eventually got used to it, but no. It grated on my nerves all year long, and I admit I did not learn as much as I should have because I desperately tried to tune the poor lady out. ~ AnnMarie

We cannot deny that our voices make a difference in what and how students learn. But who has ever talked to you about it? Have your students mentioned anything to you that you may have disregarded?

Truly, voice is extremely important. My voice, for example, changes entirely too much. I dread speaking in front of groups because I know it's not pleasant to listen to. It definitely invokes questions (i.e., Do you always sound like that? Why does your voice do that?).

I squeak.

Voices that are squeaky, that constantly change tone, that are gravelly, nasal, or that never change . . . well, these traits definitely can throw a classroom aura out of whack.

Though if you do have a voice that you KNOW is not right for the classroom, use it to your advantage. Try to make a joke out of it, or a game, or a reward. I told my students, "If you can remember the sentence I spoke without squeaking, you get a homework pass!"

We all have faults and students understand this, but trying to hide them or not acknowledging them—that's just asking for chaos and disruption in a classroom. ~ AnnMarie

Notice the transparent acknowledgment of a (potential) shortcoming. The idea of a reward was an excellent example of how to transparently convey a sense of humility.

I jumped for joy when I read this section! I really hope that teachers will un-derstand the importance of the teacher's physical voice in the classroom. The kids responded well to my ability to speak expressively, and rarely did I have discipline problems while teaching.

At one point, my husband received orders for a new base, and we had to move halfway through the year. They found the new teacher in December, and she was to work with me until I left in February. We shared teaching time. The students were so used to my animated delivery that when the new teacher taught, you could see their minds shut off. She was very monotone and couldn't understand why she couldn't hold their attention.

How do you tell someone it's because of her voice? ~ *Tori*

Many teachers have difficulty with management largely due to the lack of vocal training, which translates into less learning. It may seem strange and artificial to talk about it, particularly for veteran teachers. Is this tool of the teacher persona holding us back from effective classroom management? We've all taken public speaking, probably. But where did we need to improve? Do you remember what your evaluators said about your voice?

A "Teacher Voice" for high schoolers is lower than a normal speaking voice. A lower pitch generally carries farther and is far richer. It has more depth and resonance. This doesn't mean we shouldn't vary inflection (the up and down of the voice), however. Nor does it mean we can't change the volume or pitch (the high or low).

However, when we do change volume or pitch, it should be done for—you've probably guessed it—*emphasis*. Additionally, speaking clearly is always advisable.

For both men and women, a lower pitch is more soothing. You can tell if you're working in a deeper pitch if you can feel vibrations in your chest when you talk. You're using more of your lungs, so these vibrations will carry out into the air, leading to a richer sensation for the ear.

The best way to determine what you need to work on is to record yourself talking. Record yourself three times: (1) having a simple conversation with someone else; (2) reading a book aloud; and (3) giving a mock ten-minute lecture. Each instance of talking will show you a different component of your voice.

When listening to the conversation, focus on *speed*. How fast do you talk? Do you mumble?

When listening to the read-aloud, focus on whether or not you have a nasal tone. For whatever reason, if we're going to go nasal, it will be when we're reading aloud.

Listen for that monotone, especially towards the end of the lecture. Monotone occurs when we are tired, bored, or repetitive.

After you've made your recordings and observations, go back and record yourself reading or lecturing until *you* are pleased with the results—until your voice sounds pleasant, clear, and rich to *you*. You may be surprised by the effort it takes in breathing. Try using a lower tone. A friend may also be able to help out. Have him/her listen to both sets of recordings and give you some criticism.

Yes, this is an awful experience, but if improving our vocal technique will somehow, some way, improve student behavior and bring us closer to our ideal class, then it is worth the time, effort, and torture!

> *Your voice was simple authority. I respected you from day one, and it is because of how you used the level of your voice to regain control of a room.*
> *(Note: Now this isn't to say Ms. K couldn't yell, so when she did, I knew she meant business.)*
> *But in no way did I find your voice nasal or squeaky; I found it calming. You were able to exercise a tight control while lecturing, relax during the intimate (and heated) AP discussions, and banter with us before class in a variety of accents for emphasis. You could speak teenager (whether you thought you could or not)!* ~ Crystal

The goal is for students to determine that their teacher's voice is pleasant, interesting, and easy to understand. If we are serious about our craft, we will do whatever it takes to get there. This might seem like a small, inconsequential thing to do, but the data is in: the Teacher Voice is an important instrument of conveyance of our persona.

THE AUTHENTIC SMILE:
THE HEART OF THE TEACHER PERSONA

Ah, the smiling debate. Opponents of smiling assert that by smiling we are, somehow, sending out a signal of weakness or passivity. They cite that the moment they drop their guard and smile, especially if done so at any moment prior to winter break, the dark portal of Hades opens right there in the classroom.

Consider that, possibly, the smile was not used appropriately or consistently to begin with; thus, it was a signal to the students: "Hey, Teacher is going to let us get away with some craziness, today! He/she is in a 'good' mood!"

> *If the smile is genuine, and yet the teacher maintains the strength and authority of his/her voice, then I can't see how it could be harmful to the class. Any repercussions, such as students believing the teacher will go easy on them on any particular occasion, are not likely to be the result of a smile alone.* ~ Daniel

A smile equals neither weakness nor lack of authority. If used appropriately and consistently, a smile will take you further with students than anything else. It should not represent your *mood*; rather, it should represent your *professionalism*.

Should the expectations of professionalism and warmth for teachers be any less than those expectations of someone in any other industry that depends on cooperation and collaboration?

The smile alone, though, is not enough. It must be accompanied by sincere, authentic eye contact because the eyes confirm the authenticity of the smile. A false smile is offered without the eyes confirming it, so for the purposes of our definition, the use of smile denotes an *authentic* smile.

Young people can always tell the difference between a real smile and a fake smile. I think the older we get, the more we lose that sense of discernment. Kids can always snoop out insincerity. It's a gift! ~ Christina

The ability to choose the best and most appropriate time to smile is what conveys that warmth. Purposefully smiling at students, when greeting or saying good-bye, makes sense. Purposefully smiling when you see them in the hall emphasizes your connection and relationship with them.

From there, smile when it seems appropriate to do so: in appreciation, in humility, in acknowledgment, and in fun. But, more importantly, understand how that smile impacts classroom management.

Most days you did have a smile on your face, and it was obvious that the smile was authentic. People automatically feel more at ease around a person who is smiling—perhaps that's why so many students opened up in your class and participated? ~ Christina

So, what matters is that *when* we smile, it must be transparently real. It stands for validation of something the student says or does. It stands for acknowledgment of their presence. It stands for a sense of togetherness. It only means something *positive*.

What we shouldn't do is use it as a weapon of condescension or sarcasm. Of course, we know that already. However, it doesn't seem to stop us. There's nothing more belittling than the smug smile a teacher bestows on a student who has given an incorrect answer. The message seems to be: "You're sooooo wrong, and I'm sooooo right."

There's also the smile of power, another weapon. This is a smile of satisfaction that precedes a disciplinary step. The thinking is, "Gotcha!" This misuse of one of the most powerful nonverbal communication tools teachers possess is a travesty: a cold, joyful revenge.

Finding out how you use your smile may entail asking a colleague to observe you, or perhaps, if you're permitted, you can videotape yourself. Yes, this is another torture (I'd rather swim with piranhas), this watching of yourself on video. It might hurt, but it's you. It's really *you*. Watching yourself and evaluating yourself is yet another way to become more comfortable with yourself.

It's also a lesson in humility. Everyone has room to improve somewhere, whether it's the voice or the smile. Getting over yourself and your pride and fear *now* will help you reach your goals with students.

Ask your colleague (or you can observe from the video) to tick the number of times you smile, identifying the ones that seem to be authentic. Ask him/her to identify any *negative* uses of smiling: are you gloating, for example? Are you laughing at a student? This may be unconscious behavior, so don't dismiss the possibility that you're using your smile incongruously.

A smile has the ability to empower, motivate, and connect. It is a reassurance of acceptance, contentment, and control that students need. As a previous administrator once noted on an observation, "You cover your class with a warm blanket."

That blanket was the effective use of a smile. As we begin to use these tools properly, our ideal class is one step closer.

BUSINESS DRESS: THE EXTERNAL
COMMUNICATION OF TEACHER PERSONA

How we dress impacts student behavior, particularly at the secondary level. Consider that these students are the fashionistas of the next generation! We are constantly subjected to scrutiny, judged, and tagged.

You may think appropriate apparel is a no-brainer. Of course, we're all aware of what business dress, casual business dress, casual-Friday dress is. However, for all that we judge students by their sagging pants, low-rise jeans, and scene clothes, we must also judge ourselves.

> *If a student is going to look up to anyone, it should at least be someone who looks the part. Teachers should be comfortable, of course, but should also have a degree of dignity to set them apart. ~ Daniel*

If you desire to be taken as a professional, a mentor, and a role model, it means you have to dress professionally. Dignity is not achieved by wearing expensive clothing, but by dressing as best suited to your weight, height, and age. Make no mistake: how a high school teacher dresses makes a difference in the class's behavior.

For men, this doesn't seem to be as much of a problem. As long as your clothes fit properly (neither too tight nor too loose—take a look) and are pressed, clean, and mended, you are all set.

It wouldn't hurt some gentlemen to consider colors other than navy, tan, white, and black, but guys, you've got it easy. You may want to check on the standard tie width every other year or so, however, and tie clips always provide a nice polish. A floppy tie is distracting and somewhat undignified.

Gals, we have more of a dilemma: how to dress *comfortably*, while still dressing professionally. Watching some of those makeover reality shows can help us determine what's best for our respective body types. For example, the "apple" body type (such as this author's) has no business wearing anything constrictive, let alone rayon-spandex.

Younger ladies, you have it exceptionally tough. You still have the figure to show off! The challenge, though, is to model professionalism in your dress. You know you've got the legs, but where does your skirt wind up when you sit down? You may have beautiful curves, but is it necessary to wear skin-tight pants? Can the students tell what type of undergarments you're wearing or lack of same?

One teacher I knew had what the guys would call a "rockin' body"—she often wore outfits that showed her curves and high heels that were undoubtedly uncomfortable by the time lunch rolled around. There were many outfits that she wore that I don't know if I'd ever wear to church. ~ *Christina*

Definitely consider that the shoes you wear are probably the most important item in your wardrobe. Are your high heels killing you by the end of the day, thus making you a bit crankier? How your feet feel impacts your entire body. As a single item, they are the single most important purchase you'll make for the school year. We are of no benefit looking fabulous but feeling bad.

Consider the message we send to students when we wear well-fitted business apparel, hose, and business heels: "My teacher cares about herself and her job."

This is a subtle way to convey self-confidence, but again consider our goal: the ideal class experience. Our mode of dress is well within our control and perhaps, the quickest way to enhance our transparent purpose for being there!

The message we send by dressing professionally will, at the very least, send an alternative to the current pop culture media hype that teachers are either "geeky" and "dumpy" or "too sexy," neither of which are desirable looks in professionals.

If you're at a loss, consult a friend whose style you really like, but consider your apparel as one of the ways to convey your teacher persona effectively. It is one of the tangible ways to move towards that ideal class.

POTPOURRI: OTHER EXTERNAL
ISSUES TO CONSIDER

*I'd often find myself intently listening on in bewilderment to a teacher's peculiar
vocal mannerisms, while somehow avoiding gleaning any pertinent information
from the lesson. ~ Daniel*

One helpful aspect of videotaping yourself is that you can rewind and watch
the same presentation from another perspective. You can view it specifically
towards assessing your mannerisms, body language, and other quirks.

Mannerisms

We may or may not be aware of our mannerisms. When was the last time we
asked anyone to evaluate us from this perspective?

I had one student tell me I looked like I had flippers instead of arms.
He then proceeded to demonstrate with an exaggerated (and humorous)
dramatic interpretation. Apparently, I held my elbows to my sides and only
used my hands and wrists for gesturing. The result was, yeah, I looked like
I had flippers.

*It does make a difference! The small, physical mannerisms are more obscure,
and I don't think they affect too much so long as the rest of the persona is strong.
Gestures and crossing the arms can be ignored with a solid vocalization, or
even a proper smile.*

*Vocal mannerisms, however, have much more of an impact. I've had teachers
that add "uhh" or "okay" to every sentence. Considering that the students are
often silent while the teacher addresses them, vocal mannerisms are far more
noticeable, and they can be very distracting. Such mannerisms also give away
that the teacher may be uncomfortable, which can seriously hinder the learning
environment. ~ Daniel*

Some mannerisms to consider are:

Twirling/flipping your hair
Playing with a necklace or keys
Licking your fingers to turn a page
Clearing your throat every two seconds
Rubbing your face, nose, eyes
Snorting derisively
Twitching your nose
Beginning sentences with "okay"
Ums and ahs

These are unconscious mannerisms because, of course, we wouldn't do them otherwise. Everyone does *something*, so it's best to be aware of whatever it is. Mannerisms are also a distracting resource for student entertainment (and future comedians) and as such, eliminating the distractions will help the students focus.

Body Language

More than likely, you studied a few tidbits on the importance of body language during your education courses or perhaps, in a teacher-preparation program. Again, the video or the observation is the best way to identify what you're doing well and what you can still work on.

The strongest negative body language is the arms crossed at the chest. It seems to be an automatic response to indicate that one is waiting. We may not intend it to be intimidating; however, it's a form of pressure.

Another possibility is that you may be using this posture as a way to de-emphasize yourself. You "cover" yourself or shut yourself "off" to allow the other person the spotlight, but unfortunately, it's not received that way. It is perceived as a position of anger/frustration, so the response to it will be either confrontation or fear. Students are either going to shut down (not talk) or strive to posture in reaction (become belligerent).

As adults, we may or may not shut down when an authority figure presents this body language, but we are not in the same frame of mind as teenagers. They still see us as authority *figures*, whether they respect us as such or not. Thus, their response to this generally negative body language will almost always be negative.

Hands on the hips is another overused stance. Again, most teachers are simply looking for a comfortable way to stand. However, it is also perceived negatively. Is this your *default* position? Do you use your body language negatively?

Flipper Epilogue: I chose to tell the class that I was working on avoiding my flippering, and they could send me a flipper signal if they saw me doing it. Eventually, I realized I was resorting to this mannerism when I was trying to get through information quickly. I still struggle with it, but I'm aware of it.

Have you got the guts to let students know you're working on something that might be distracting to them? How comfortable are you with your weaknesses? Do you feel you might lose authority by bringing this up? Consider this message that you could send to students: "My teacher knows she is not perfect, but she diligently works at improving herself."

That might not seem like a huge message to send, but it models what we expect from students: don't fear imperfection, work on it.

Watch your videotape, or simply ask your students what you do that may be distracting. By doing so, you'll improve your rapport with them. They love to judge and criticize—what adolescent doesn't?—so they'll be happy to throw in their two cents. But along the way, they'll see a person who continuously strives to improve. Humility, in this instance, will create a bond that only an ideal class can have.

This is a lot to consider. You've been asked to visualize your ideal class as a foundation. That part was probably fun! Then, you considered how comfortable you are with your *self* because that comfort will lay the foundation for your class. Moreover, you've pondered over your ability to be humble and transparently convey yourself as a student/learner as a means to bring you closer to your vision. Finally, you took a look at how you physically and externally present yourself in the classroom, which is an uncomfortable area of criticism.

You may be thinking, "Great Giblet's Ghost! This is already too much to think about! I've got a class to teach, and I can't be worrying about whether I'm smiling or not!"

Yes, you've got a class to teach. And the more *aware* you become while doing it, the more you will bring your students into the experience. The more you convey comfort and humility as a learner, the more effective you will be.

One final note from me: force nothing. In being humble and establishing a persona that works with students, authenticity is key. Nothing can destroy an attempt at being genuine like forcing your behavior patterns. People aren't perfect, and a teacher needs to accept who he/she is.

A teacher can adjust and adapt using the tips given here without creating a persona that's contrary to the self. Doing so means establishing a genuine bond. Forcing the creation of a contradictory persona will prevent bonds from being formed and sever those that have already been made. ~ Daniel

Our next chapters highlight the practical, logistical steps you will take, using your vision and transparent teacher persona. With this philosophy behind you, your students will follow you to the ideal class. And you? You will LOVE your job.

Chapter Four

Your Classroom
Management Begins Now

WHAT TO DO BEFORE THE RUSH

I had one classroom management class, but the focus was on theorists and their theories. I don't feel our textbook was 100 percent the answer for understanding management. ~ Stacey

Current courses provide new teachers with an excellent overview of theories, but the application of those same theories is a practical experience. The discussion of *how* is often vague. Additionally, understanding that classroom management begins *before* the school year even starts can make a huge difference in how students receive their teachers.

Educators exhaust themselves in explaining their use of time to those out of (and in) the field of education. Simply put, the hours teachers put into the task of teaching far exceed their contractual expectations or obligations. Who knows of any teacher who is able to do the job without putting in some personal time? (It would be interesting for someone to gauge the correlation between outside hours worked and student achievement. Any takers?)

One of the things people don't realize when stepping into a teacher's shoes is its impact on the other aspects of your life. Working within constraints and maximizing use of time is the ultimate goal, and had I read this book before going into the classroom, I would have had a much better understanding of managing that time. ~ AnnMarie

I can't even count how many hours I put in during my first year of teaching and beyond. All the "extra" hours did have an impact, not only on students' behavior but also in their learning environment—ultimately leading to their achievement. ~ Tori

Preparation outside of contracted days and hours might seem extreme. The argument might be, "I work like a dog during the school year, so my time off is my time off. Period."

But what if doing *some* preparation during the summer—unencumbered with deadlines and stress—meant that you would have an easier time during the school year? What if a few hours during the summer meant *less* time during the school year? How might that impact the daily stresses you know are coming up?

How many *extra* hours do you put in every week during the school year? Five? Ten? If you deduce that you'll be putting in some hours above and beyond, then *when* and *how* you put in those hours should be up to you. How we approach this time, all the planning, researching, and so on, is our choice. Most people, we can safely assume, do their best work when neither stressed nor overwhelmed.

Finally, you might also want to consider that you begin to model your expectations of students with these preparation tactics. For example, when we give students a month to complete a project or big assignment, we expect to see evidence that the student has spent some quality time and effort, correct? Here is an opportunity to model that expectation and walk your talk.

For new teachers, it's important that you understand the *types* of time that teaching entails before moving into the logistics of it. Veteran teachers certainly understand what's coming up, but viewing teaching time through this lens of separation may be helpful.

A positive experience for the students is a positive experience for the teacher. A bit of planning outside school hours can go a long way towards that end. That extra effort will make the job more pleasant for all which, in turn, will make the additional preparation seem less like a chore. ~ Daniel

DIVISIONS OF TIME

Mandatory (Inside) Hours aka *Contractual Hours*

This category refers to the contractual hours, and includes pre-service days, teacher work days, and planning periods. The bulk of these hours, though, are *instructional hours*: the specific class periods you spend with students.

In the first years of teaching, instructional hours can be overwhelming. Most stress occurs during this time, depending on student behavior or "how the class goes."

You might also feel buried by administrative tasks, which take up a good bit (if not all) of the remaining mandatory hours. These tasks include attending meetings, inputting data/grades, and completing forms. The question becomes: what can be done during "outside" hours to offset this stress during "inside" hours?

Mandatory (Outside) Hours aka *Not Contracted*

This category refers to any time that an educator might spend on the completion of required certification/training, in paid extracurricular sports/clubs, or serving the school as a whole.

Although many in-services provide teachers with a nice head start towards recertification, inevitably, we're going to have to do something extra and on our own time. Taking online courses for a required additional certification, while still trying to teach classes, can be a train wreck. However, choosing *when* to take courses (usually) is your own decision. How might you handle this facet of the job better?

Coaching a sport or sponsoring a club is a valuable contribution to students. First-year teachers should choose very carefully before signing up for anything. The stipends are compelling, but usually don't correspond to the amount of time you will spend in either of these activities. If you're in your first year, consider holding off until you've got one year under your belt. Veteran teachers should evaluate whether they are overdoing.

Also, we are always encouraged to volunteer or lead committees. Can administrators actually *force* you to do any of these? No. The encouragement will be very, very strong, though, and intense enough (perhaps) to merit placement in this mandatory category.

For example, we all want to be a part of the improvement or the betterment of the school, so serving on any number of committees may beckon you. However, you may soon find yourself hopping from meeting to meeting. Your dedication is undeniable, but your follow-through might be sporadic. How can you do this and not be too tired to stay focused on your primary tasks?

Choice (Outside) Hours aka *Your Time*

Any class stuff that you don't have time to complete during the day or time spent volunteering with students on projects, sports, or clubs might be part of your *choice* hours. These unpaid sponsorships are a wonderful experience, but you'll want to assess whether (or to what extent) they are negatively impacting your work in the classroom.

Planning and grading probably weigh in the heaviest for outside hours. Although most schools still offer a planning period, the time provided pathetically skims the surface of what is actually needed to meet the goals presented.

Vertical teaming, writing grants, and working with colleagues just take more time than is offered contractually.

For example, you might want to research new ways to teach a certain aspect of your course. Anyone who has done research on the Internet can attest to how much time it sucks up—you follow a trail of enticing web crumbs, and four hours have passed before you know it!

On any given week, you'll make it through the *inside* hours, but the load of administrative expectations and coursework of the *outside* hours may be the source of your stress. Here's what you need to do to ensure that you spend your time effectively and in the way you desire to spend it!

PREEMPTIVE MANAGEMENT

You're probably going to put in those few extra hours, so make darn sure you do so on your terms. Here's where preemptive management comes in. It is the *shifting* of time so that a considerable portion of planning and parent contact occurs prior to the school year.

Yes, this means doing some things during the summer. Yes, this is your vacation. However, those summer hours that you put in definitively correlate to a year's worth of a smoother, more valuable learning experience for students. In other words, the payoff is more than worth it.

In the corporate world, there is an implied trust when giving managers a salary: a salary means that one works until the job is done, no matter how long it takes. That same logic can work for the teaching world. After all, we are not paid *by the hour*; we are on a contract for a *salary*. How you spend the equivalent of your ten months' salary is your business.

Even if it means spending a bit of time outside of the established time frame, when you put in a more concerted effort prior to the school year, then *you* will be the one walking around on teacher workdays asking other teachers if they need help with anything. Your work will be *done*.

Other teachers may shake their head and say, "You'll burn out. You're doing too much."

Well, no, you're not doing *more*; you're doing the same thing they are, just *more effectively*. You might even hear, "You're making the rest of us look bad. Stop it."

What these folks don't get is that while they are tearing their hair out midyear, you'll be on the downhill slope, enjoying the ride! Wouldn't you rather start off strong and have the time to enjoy yourself the remainder of the year? *How* you spend your outside hours and *when* you spend them is your choice.

Yes, this is your holiday. Yes, you'll putter around a bit in your classroom during the summer. However, by doing so, you'll love your job, so you'll love preparing for it. Step one of preparation?

Step One: Do Nothing

Step One, the sweet art of doing nothing, isn't easy, especially if you have a child or children, a house to clean, doctors' appointments, vet appointments, and all that stuff that you didn't do during the school year because you didn't have time.

You'll want to be very strict about your Nothing Time. The first year of trying out this method, go for the first two weeks after school ends. Every year after that, your Nothing Time will extend a bit longer as you streamline the entire process. Doing nothing includes:

Staying off the computer
Not talking about school
Not thinking about school
Not reading about education
Not taking any classes
Not watching any movies or TV shows that have anything to do with education
Doing only what you want to do
Understanding what "have to do" really means
Not taking a vacation (just yet)

Stepping away from a computer for two weeks may seem like utter madness. However, if you want to love your job, then you are going to have to do nothing. The computer may be our entertainment or our connection to the world, but it is also a brain drain. You need to recharge.

- Tell your social network friends you're stepping away for two weeks. They *will* survive without your posts.
- Send out a group e-mail to let people know: *I'm out for two weeks, but you can call me.*
- Online games are great distractions, but you can't taste the sweetness of nothing if you're piddling around for game badges.

This will be difficult at first. However, you'll soon find that you have a few extra moments to spend with your family, children, dog. You'll begin to taste the sweetness.

Not talking about school can be difficult, especially if you're talking to a fellow colleague. You'll have to make a conscious effort to say, "Oops! Hold on! I'm not talking about school until June __. I'm taking a break! You should, too!"

If you happen to see students while you're out, consciously keep the discussion on summer things: vacations, the beach, and so on. If they start to talk about school or class, gently lead them to another topic.

Not *thinking* about school is a little trickier, but do your best. Following the list above can help you out because if you're not reading about education, you may actually think about something else.

When you don't know what day of the week it is, you're on the right track. When you take the time to make coffee in a French press, indulge in chocolate-chip pancakes, or read the paper (avoiding the education section) while listening to Gershwin after rising at the glorious hour of 10 a.m., you have tasted the sweetness of doing nothing. Head to the beach or a pool. Putter around the closets.

You are more than "school" or "class" or "students." You are someone who enjoys other things: sports, reading, music, walking, cooking, collecting, friends, films, conversation, barbecues, museums. Try to catch hold of that person you were *before* becoming a teacher for these two weeks. By doing so, you will put yourself into a position of *wanting* to begin your planning, and that desire makes all of the difference.

> *Holding on to one's identity can prove immensely valuable in forming and preserving a strong bond between teacher and student. Forget who you are, become merely a teacher with no other existence, and that's all the students will ever see.*
>
> *Students, who are quick to disassociate themselves from a "teacher," find it more difficult to disassociate from someone with an actual character. I responded more positively to a person than I did to a nebulous entity rooted solely in a title.* ~ *Daniel*

For the naysayers currently revving up your engines, your questions probably revolve around the things you "hafta" (have to) do. The only time you have for annual physical exams and dentist appointments (and so on) is during the summer.

"There's just not enough time to get things done in the summer! How can I take two weeks and just do *nothing*?" you keen.

The idea is not to forgo these haftas; the idea is simply to *not* make appointments for the first two weeks. You can get by making nonemergency appointments ahead of time for week three or beyond.

Do what you want to do and in the order you want to do it. The philosophy is simple: whatever you can get away with *not* doing for those two weeks, don't. Determining what a hafta actually is may take a few moments of consideration. Ask yourself:

If I *wait* to do this, will someone or I be physically or emotionally hurt?

If I *wait* to do this, will someone or I suffer in some way (e.g., not going to the market for groceries/not getting car repaired)?

This two-pronged test works pretty well. If something *can* wait until you've finished your two weeks' respite, then it should wait. Let your family be aware of the necessity of these two weeks for you.

Often, older parents are part of our equation as well as children, and they can be equally demanding. It's difficult, but you'll have to be a little tough. Mom might demand that she wants you to go with her for whatever outing, but if you don't *want* to go, tell her that you're doing something for school. That something is *nothing*.

Step Two: Preemptive Communication

(*Note:* Do not begin Step Two without completing Step One or a version of it, if at all possible.)

Of all the steps you can take prior to pre-service days, this one will make the most difference in preempting potential classroom management issues. Effective classroom management doesn't begin the first day of school. It begins approximately two weeks prior to teacher pre-service days, or roughly three weeks before the start of school. It begins by establishing a rapport with the student and parent.

> *Having a daughter in high school now, it seems like the teachers of today are not as involved in their students' lives as they were when we were in school. My daughter is in her third year of high school and has never mentioned any of her teachers in such a manner as I would have "back in the day." I have asked her on occasion who her favorite teacher is or was, and sadly, her reply has been "No one really." ~ Parent*

This is your chance to begin becoming involved. If your district permits off-site web access to the database, pull your schedules and students. Or, take a trip to the school to download what you need. Either way, get your list of students and print their contact info—one page per student will help you create your contact log. Hopefully, your administration has students registered in courses early. Bless you, guidance departments!

If you don't know when the master schedule is completed, it's worth a call to find out and plan your trip. (As some schools don't have schedules done until the first day of school, you'll want to pay special attention to the Cramming It All In section.)

Granted, these will be rough schedules, and of course, some students might be moved in or out. However, with this *basic* registry of students, you can begin introductory calls.

Most schools desire that teachers communicate with parents, but they don't necessarily provide a solid strategy or protocol for doing so. Your goal is to contact every parent and student prior to the school year. By doing so, you'll begin to establish a rapport with each student and a *positive* relationship with the parent(s) or guardian.

The first call to any parent should not be to discuss a problem with the student; rather, it should be a congenial and enthusiastic meeting of minds. Moreover, this call provides parents with answers to questions they might have concerning necessary supplies or dates for events. You're an ambassador for the school! Project professionalism and concern.

Welcome calls

These calls generally take no more than ten to fifteen minutes each. Work class by class, alphabetically, until you've exhausted at least three attempts to reach each student at different times of the day/week. As you make each attempt, you might want to log the attempt information at the bottom of the page, for example:

- NA: no answer
- LM: left message
- W#: wrong number
- #OOS: number out of service

Once you make contact with the parent, consider covering the following points:

- Self-introduction
- Verification of contact information
- Getting an e-mail address for both parent and student (if applicable)
- General course overview
- Supplies needed for the course (if any)
- Info on Open House night (always encouraging parents to come)
- Your contact information for parents (always encouraging communication at any time)

It's important to let the parent drive the call because you'll gain more valuable information that way. (See Figure 4.1 for a sample parent call script.) Many times parents will have questions or offer information that might lead the call.

From these early conversations, you'll find out that David has a reading problem or Shawntae has a medical condition, information which may or may not be readily available on your contact sheet. Jot down any information you receive about the student on his/her individual printout.

Most importantly, get the parent's e-mail address! The focus is professional and courteous, and the message conveyed is, "I'm going to do my best for your child."

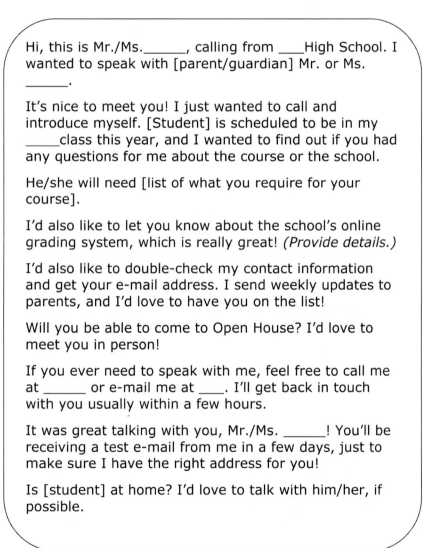

Hi, this is Mr./Ms._____, calling from ___High School. I wanted to speak with [parent/guardian] Mr. or Ms. _____.

It's nice to meet you! I just wanted to call and introduce myself. [Student] is scheduled to be in my _____class this year, and I wanted to find out if you had any questions for me about the course or the school.

He/she will need [list of what you require for your course].

I'd also like to let you know about the school's online grading system, which is really great! *(Provide details.)*

I'd also like to double-check my contact information and get your e-mail address. I send weekly updates to parents, and I'd love to have you on the list!

Will you be able to come to Open House? I'd love to meet you in person!

If you ever need to speak with me, feel free to call me at _____ or e-mail me at ___. I'll get back in touch with you usually within a few hours.

It was great talking with you, Mr./Ms. _____! You'll be receiving a test e-mail from me in a few days, just to make sure I have the right address for you!

Is [student] at home? I'd love to talk with him/her, if possible.

Figure 4.1. Sample Parent Welcome Call Script

You'll also want to ask to speak to the student if he/she is at home. Follow a similar outline, but tailor this conversation to students, asking what they like or don't like about ___ (insert your course/class). You might also find out about their goals and extracurricular activities.

If you have one really cool project that you're going to tackle during the school year, tell the student, encouraging any ideas or input for improvement. (See Figure 4.2 for a sample student call script.) The focus should always be upbeat and positive, and the message is, "I'm *excited* to have you in my class."

Hey, [student]! This is Mr./Ms._____! I'm scheduled to be your _____ teacher this year! I just wanted to introduce myself and find out if you had any questions for me about the course.

Do you like [subject]?

Do you do any clubs or sports? Your mom/dad/guardian tells me that you like _____!

We're going to be doing a lot of stuff this year, but I'm really excited about our ___project that we start in September! If you like [sports, gaming, music, certain genre of literature], I think you'll really like it!

Also, I wanted to get your e-mail address because I'm going to be sending out some e-mails from time to time about grades and stuff.

Do you think you'll be able to make it to Open House? I can't wait to meet you!

It was great talking with you, [student]! I'll see you then!

Figure 4.2. Sample Student Welcome Call Script

These days, the only time students mention their teachers to their parents is when they have a complaint. Likewise, parents often choose to act on their children's behalf, resulting in them becoming antagonistic towards the teacher.

However, a positive call (early on) allows the teacher to speak to the parent in a more rational state of mind. Creating that sort of association makes it easier to resolve potential conflicts before they happen, and towards the benefit of all involved by getting the parent to help their child as opposed to hindering the teacher. That's how important one simple call can be. ~ Daniel

How would you feel if *your* child's *high school* teacher called you with this level of professionalism? What would you think about a teacher who offered her contact information to ensure that the communication lines were open?

E-mail check

After you've collected ten or twenty e-mails, you'll want to do a test run to make sure the e-mail addresses are correct. Inevitably, you'll have to correct a typo or missing letter/digit in an address. This quick check will ensure you have the right info.

Just a simple "E-mail Check" in the subject line and "Thanks! Mr./Ms. Teacher" in the body will do the trick because you've already told the parent that you'll be doing this.

However, this first run of information ensures that you have a direct connection to parents/students for upcoming newsletters and notifications. You can run two or three "batches" as you collect the information, using only the new addresses.

You can imagine the reaction of a parent whose child's high school teacher is calling and e-mailing them. Most are genuinely surprised. *All* are pleased. This is where you can start your school year: with a positive ten-minute phone call and a quick e-mail. This is how you begin to build the ideal class.

(Total Hours Avg.: approximately twenty hours, two hours per day, based on two hundred students.)

The one thing that I felt you had that I had never experienced in another teacher, ever, was your professionalism. I remember you coming into one of my classes in tenth grade, and you handed me a welcome letter, summer assignment, and books needed for AP. I was amazed that you were already ready for next year, and it made me feel special because you came to hand me the letter personally. ~ Stacey

CRAMMING IT ALL IN

If you don't have access to your student rosters until pre-service days or the first day of school, things are going to be a bit hectic. If you find yourself in this situation, consider the following approach.

- Do not skip the Welcome calls step.
- Make phone calls starting the day you receive the information, adjusting the script accordingly.
- Complete the calls no later than the first weekend after you receive the information. Consider that this will be the best time to accomplish this task.

These calls make the difference in your students' behavior. If you make this effort a priority, you will be rewarded with an ideal class.

THE ZEN OF VISITING THE CLASSROOM IN THE SUMMER

If you are able, you may want to put in a visit to your classroom, just to putter about with whatever cannot be accomplished from home. Bring your CD player and lose yourself in organizing files, desks, cabinets, and papers. Anything you can do at home, you'll want to smoosh into a tote bag.

I loved going to my classroom early. It was so peaceful! I was only there a couple of days in total, but I was able to get a jump on the entire school year. ~ Tori

Some of your most profound observations will be made while you are alone in that room. Additionally, that feeling of accomplishment soothes stress.

This level of preparation will exponentially lessen every year as you sharpen your end-of-year process. However, a few hours working in the classroom, used wisely, allow you to appreciate and enjoy your pre-service days!

(Total Hours Avg.: five)

I like the idea of going into the classroom early because there are things you can do on your own time that do make the difference, and then you'll have less stress, less cramming during pre-service. New teachers need to do this because they have no idea how much of pre-service is spent in whole groups, data meetings, team building, and whatever-else meetings. When new teachers finally get into the classroom they have no idea where to even start! Then, you have other teachers stopping by to chit chat. Pre-service is a crazy time! I'm glad you are incorporating this because I've never seen it discussed elsewhere. ~ Stacey

A SPECIAL NOTE ABOUT TEACHER KIDS

Balancing parenthood and family time with this time at work merits notice. My son, like any other kid, hated going anywhere that might be considered "boring." However, when I recently asked him his thoughts about going to school with me in the summer (every year from age five to age twelve, he said:

> It was kinda fun because I had my games, and you let me draw on the chalkboard. Having some toys there helped. Remember we'd pack a box just for me? I had the whole classroom as a playroom, and I was spending time with you.

Generally, taking him somewhere fun afterwards (such as an arcade, park, or play-place) helped him cope, too. We had outside picnics after a morning in the class.

If you have very little ones, you may want to consider a sitter for a day. Are there other teachers who are coming in to work? Find a willing student to watch a small gaggle of children and share the cost of babysitting. Lowering your job stress will also lower your parenting stress.

My mother worked in the guidance department of a school I attended, and I often found myself staying after class in her office until she could take my sister and me home. It was tedious, but I'll never say I resented her in any way for it. It was necessary and, ultimately, not that bad, especially when she remembered a thing or two that helped alleviate any boredom. ~ Daniel

ONE WEEK BEFORE PRE-SERVICE DAYS

Student Folders

About one week before pre-service days, make photocopies and gather all relevant forms, syllabi, documents, letters, and business cards for the students. The process of making copies is stressful, isn't it? Whether it's the line of people waiting, or the fact that the machines inevitably break down during pre-service days when they are most needed, the tension is palpable. You'll find a spiritual centeredness in making your copies before pre-service days begin.

Consider preparing a folder for each student (a simple manila folder will do), with every necessary form inside. The assembly-line method is the easiest way to tackle this project: work class by class, always creating at least five complete extra folders.

The cost of folders might be a consideration, especially if your school does not provide you with supplies or those supplies are not yet available to you.

Consider reaching out to the school's established business partners for a box of folders (your assistant principal will be able to help you out) or ask for donations of manila folders from several businesses. Most businesses are willing to give you a small pile once you explain the need. The nice thing about those manila folders is that they are uniform and standard; thus, *where* you get them is arbitrary. A student folder might contain these items:

- welcome letter
- business card
- syllabus and/or course outline
- contact form
- icebreaker

Seasoned teachers also know that by the time school actually starts, another four or five administrative documents will need to be given to students. The student folders are a very simple way to maneuver this maze of paperwork and avoid the time it takes to hand everything out, piece by tedious piece.

You might also consider keeping student folders in plastic boxes with hanging files, labeled with the class period or course name, so you know which group needs what stuff. Isn't that what milk crates are made for, anyway?

Welcome Letter

The welcome letter is a nice touch for students and parents, and certainly, some never make it home. That's why the calls are beneficial. One way or the other, you're going to express your welcome. Even though you may have already spoken to parents, this letter will reiterate your enthusiasm.

It should be short, professional, and include your contact information. If possible, copy the letter onto school letterhead, which will help distinguish it from other forms. Your school secretary is a valuable ally for this sort of stuff, so introduce yourself or pay homage during the summer when he or she isn't as busy. (See Figure 4.3 for Sample Welcome Letter Introduction.) To save yourself some time, this letter should be very general, undated, and only revised if your contact information or course titles change.

Business Cards

Your peers will think you're a little crazy for giving out business cards, but if nothing else, by the first day, your students and the parents will clearly understand that you are serious about teaching their children. This card should include your business e-mail and relevant phone numbers.

Our Great High School

Dear Parent or Guardian,

I'd like to take this opportunity to welcome you and your child to my class. I am planning an exciting year for my students, and I hope that each of them enjoys the challenges and projects that lie ahead. . .

Figure 4.3. Sample Welcome Letter Introduction

Office supply stores sell rip-and-tear card sheets for a reasonable sum, or if funds are scarce, cut out business-card-sized pieces of paper, formatted *as* business cards. The message conveyed by this simple gesture is *priceless* pre-emptive classroom management: "I can reach my teacher/my child's teacher at any time."

A snarky question that you might hear is, "What about prank calls?"

Out of all the years of handing out my home phone (and later, cell phone) to students, not one parent or student took advantage of this information. Rather, you may have to remind students that if they have a question about homework—it is *okay* to call.

Is this an exercise in trust? Absolutely. But, we have to start somewhere, and at the beginning of the year is the best time.

The simplest way to avoid prank calls is to not give them the idea. Mention it, and you're asking for it! ~ Daniel

I remember the business card, and I actually called you a few times to ask homework questions. I was very nervous about bothering you after school, but I really liked knowing you were available to help me! ~ Stacey

Agreed—it's very intimidating, especially if the student hasn't had you as a teacher before. However, I suppose that's the teacher's job—to make the student realize: (a) the teacher is there to help, and (b) the teacher is the same person that the student talks to each day without hesitation. ~ Christina

THOUGHTS ON STRESS AND TIME

Even though you may be on summer break, you'll probably still experience the pressure of stress and lack of time. You might even be working a summer job! Your mind might be reeling with all of these potentially new tasks that you desire to undertake, everything mushed together in a viscous glob of *do this*.

Rather than attempting all of these tasks at once, try prioritizing and segmenting them into chunks of time. Figure 4.4 provides a general strategy and approach for completing the goals in this chapter and the following chapters.

You might be separating these tasks into hours, days, weeks, or a combination, so that's your first consideration. Regardless, your priority for every chunk is to begin with the Welcome Calls, which are the most important.

You might, using the weekly approach, do welcome calls for two days, followed by two days of syllabus development. Or, if you're using the daily approach, you might spend two chunks of time on Welcome Calls and two chunks on syllabus (which is our next chapter focus). Notice the shift of tasks as you move forward. Each day (or week) still has the main priority of Welcome Calls underscoring the focus. However, you systematically move from focus to focus.

Chunking your time accomplishes a few things: (1) you'll feel more productive; (2) you'll move forward in priority; and (3) simply having a plan helps alleviate stress.

So, the total number of outside hours for the summer so far is approximately twenty-five. You will not be remunerated, but you will feel satisfied and content. You'll have a grip on things before you've even begun! How can you put a price on this level of peace of mind? How can you place a value on less stress?

(*Note:* After using this approach for three years, my average went down to about ten hours in the summer, largely due to knowing exactly what I would say and do at any given point along the way.)

Day/Week One	Day/Week Two	Day/Week Three	Day/Week Four	Day/Week Five
Welcome Calls	*Welcome Calls*	*Welcome Calls*	*Welcome Calls*	*Welcome Calls*
Welcome Calls	*Syllabus*	*Syllabus*	*Procedures*	*Copies*
Syllabus	*Syllabus*	*Course Outline*	*Procedures*	*Copies*
Syllabus	*Course Outline*	*Course Outline*	*Supplies*	*Physical Class*

Figure 4.4. **Prioritizing Strategy**

Keep in mind, too, that *only* doing what is suggested in this chapter will only add to your total outside hours. That's certainly not what you want! However, in conjunction with the other strategies in later chapters, it actually decreases your outside time.

In other words, don't stop here just because it feels good! You want to whittle your time down to the point where you have free weekends and evening hours.

The next goal set—curriculum and planning!

Chapter Five

Making Thematic Lemonade
from Cloned Lemons

WHAT TO DO WITH PREDETERMINED
SYLLABI AND OTHER SYLLABI TIPS

*I threw away most of my syllabi throughout the course of my education, but I did
keep a few, based on one simple criterion: whether or not my teacher seemed
intent on using it.*

*If the teacher seemed to go through the motions by either droning the syllabus
out loud word for word, or by allowing the students to participate in reciting the
monotonous litany, then it became drawing paper.*

*But if the teacher addressed the syllabus as an actual framework for the
course of the class, I paid attention and held onto it throughout the course of
the year as a guide to determine where I was, where I'd gone, and where I had
yet to go. ~ Daniel*

Your district may or may not require a syllabus for your course. You'll still
want to create one, if only for your benefit and your students' benefit. Working through the academic year in this rough format will not only give you a
sense of purpose, but will also provide you with a sense of the *whole* of the
upcoming course, which is crucial in achieving your vision. It will also help
you determine how to make connections throughout the year, one of the more
difficult aspects of curriculum planning.

Our primary focus for this chapter is to work through what's handed
down from the district or state level to create a syllabus that will meet your
personal vision for the class. We hope you find a few helpful nuggets to
consider along the way, even if you're lucky enough to be creating your
own syllabus.

*For new teachers, predetermined syllabi would be beneficial—a guideline of
where to begin and how. For veteran teachers, however, this is probably like
wearing a belt that is too small! ~ Christina*

Prefabricated Syllabi

There it is, an exhaustive list of stuff to "cover" for the year, the semester, the
week, and perhaps the day, all of which is subject to change at any moment in
the most generic cookie-cutter fashion conceivable: our district-wide syllabus.
These are our restrictions and limitations. (Fighting this system warrants another
book, so let's work from the premise that this is just the way things are.)

Gah! A sense of despair sets in—there's no way to do all of this. There's
no way to get all of this "in" in time for benchmark/state standards testing.
The sheer volume of information is enough to make you ill.

Take a deep breath. We'll move section by section.

Your district (or school) has told you what they expect from you as it pertains to main assignments and units. Now, your goal is to make that expectation more personal, student-driven, and authentic. *Essentially, more . . . you!*
~ Christina

Handing students a copy of the district syllabus without truly personalizing
it is a management issue waiting to happen. It sends a horrible message: "You
are not worth my time." How do you feel when you get a form letter from a
big company? Same idea.

*I take issue with this, though. I know that a preformatted syllabus (or anything
for that matter) can seem cold and unprepared, but I would much rather have
that than nothing. Many teachers don't even take the time to give the student
any intro to what will be covered during the year. I like to know that the teacher
at least looked at what's coming up him/herself. And even if they just copy and
print it, they still have to read through it. ~ AnnMarie*

*Yes, but many teachers I had would distribute that "basic" syllabus and then,
"basically" ignore it, making the whole thing pointless. As a result, the objectives outlined in that original syllabus were rarely met. Those objectives that
were met forced students to suddenly work towards that standard without ad-
equate preparation.*

*Personalizing that syllabus can make both the teacher and students more
cognizant of the expectations placed upon them. By using and crafting a personalized framework, whether district-led or not, transitions between lessons and
objectives will be easier on everyone. ~ Daniel*

(*Note:* In the event that your district only wants you to hand the students an
exact copy of this prefab syllabus, consider crafting an addendum that is more
student friendly as an attachment.)

A syllabus is a sort of contract between the teacher, the students, and the students' parents. However, it is also a contract between the educator and the district, more so now than ever before.

Ultimately, the goal is to make this very unwieldy document into something that can be *understood* by students and parents and can be *used* throughout the school year to support your individual vision for the class.

A prefab syllabus may or may not have sections that you can "fill in," but for the most part, all curriculum and curriculum flow is prescribed by the powers that be. Very well! Your gut might be telling you:

> What's the point? All the district cares about is that we splosh this out there for students and parents. They don't care if we've gone to any trouble to reformat or personalize to any degree. So, why should I bother, when I have so many more important things to worry about? And, hey, won't handing out the prefab save me time in the long run?

It's your choice, of course. You could opt out of this component, with the idea that in other areas, you will excel.

Consider your expectations of your students' work, though, when making this choice. If you gave students a similar assignment—a "Make This Thing Your Own" assignment—what would you expect from them? More than likely, you'd want them to take the assignment seriously, giving it their best effort, even though they might see it as busy work.

Whatever you'd want from your students, that is what you'll want to give here. Give everything you've got, and they will be more inclined to follow in your footsteps. Just as you are able to see when students exert effort on an assignment, your students will be able to see your effort. Additionally, you'll naturally be more engaged and excited because you will have had a hand (somewhat) in the creation of this contract.

Yes! I had teachers that did the bare minimum—we all knew it. I had teachers that did less than the minimum—we all knew it. And guess what? I had teachers that went above and beyond—and yep, we all knew it. Those were the teachers we wanted. ~ AnnMarie

Phase One: Reformatting and Meeting Expectations

• *Step One: Identify Spots for Individuality*

First, get a copy of your district's syllabus for your course. More than likely, it's on the district website. Copy/paste the prefab syllabus into your own working document. That way, you have the option to change the font and the formatting as long as you stay true to the content.

This may not seem like much, but the more we can individualize this monster, the better off we are. What student will pay attention to a document that resembles every other teacher's document? If the teacher pays no attention to it, why should the student?

The syllabus is one of the first impressions students receive of the teacher, so the first judgment that happens in our minds is: is the syllabus personalized? Creative?

Does it say, "Hey, I'm here for you! I know this is dry material, but I promise to make it worthwhile!" Or does it say, "This is what I was given. This is what we're going over. Deal with it."? ~ Christina

Have some fun centering and formatting to your preferences. Move a bit of information here and there, but do not delete. Graphically, work towards a final product that meets *your* standards.

How you present your syllabus and your course title, particularly, is a part of classroom management. What kind of teacher persona do you want to convey? Font formats, particularly for the title of the course, can reflect your persona. A lot depends on your specific course, but it also depends on you. Which font format screams "you"?

• *Step Two: Maintaining and Rephrasing*

The wording on prefab syllabi sometimes leaves much to be desired. As long as you maintain the gist of the content, you can revise to craft a stronger syllabus for its intended audience: *the student*. Figure 5.1 shows how you might tackle this revision.

Many teachers loathe the whole process of creating a syllabus, claiming it to be the most hypocritical of actions.

"Never use 'em anyway. Just going to throw them away," they mumble, going through the motions of handing them out as required. That attitude, whether we say it out loud or not, permeates the action, negating the entire purpose of a syllabus.

Students do read them, despite what teachers may think! ~ Christina

If the syllabus is created *for* the students, then they are less likely to dispose of it. It's not that they can't understand the "educationese" presented in the prefab syllabus, it just doesn't resonate with them. Does it resonate with you? Which syllabus motivates you to teach, and which one gives you a migraine? Once students realize that this document is a useful resource

Pre-Fab	Revised
Course Content: The purpose of this course is to provide integrated educational experiences in the language arts strands of reading, writing, listening, viewing, speaking, language, and literature. The content should include, but not be limited to, the following: --using reading strategies to construct meaning from informative, technical, and literary texts --acquiring an extensive vocabulary through reading, discussion, listening, and systematic word study --using process writing strategies, student inquiry, and self-monitoring techniques --using speaking, listening, and viewing strategies in formal presentations and informal discussions	**Course Content:** English Two will provide you with experience in all of the language arts strands (reading, writing, listening, viewing, speaking, language, and literature). We'll be doing a lot of different things! The course will include all of this (and, probably, more!): • using reading strategies to understand meaning • building vocabulary through reading, discussion, listening • using writing strategies, research strategies, and self-monitoring techniques • using speaking, listening, and viewing strategies in presentations and informal discussions

Figure 5.1. Wording Syllabus for Students

that you consistently use, then you'll reap the numerous rewards of taking this time to do it.

• *Step Three: Emphasizing Your Vision*

The one area on a prefab syllabus that seems to be the most flexible for teachers (still) is logistical management. We still seem to have some ability to choose *how* we want the students to present their work (i.e., folders/binders), and we also have some degree of flexibility as it pertains to expectations. These areas of the syllabus, then, should clearly reflect your persona and vision.

So many teachers use a syllabus that is "generic" or used year after year. When the syllabus speaks to us as students, we are more inclined to listen to you, the teacher. While working on this, I actually found a copy of my Drama II syllabus. I've kept it all this time—close to thirteen years! It still has my notes! ~ Christina

The *Star Trek* font in this syllabus (Figure 5.2) immediately tells the students a few things: this instructor is a *Star Trek* fan, possibly a little on the geeky side, but not afraid to be creative. Graphically, it's formatted in a pleasing way,

---

ᗡRAMA TWO SYLLABUS
Fall/Spring Semesters 99-00
MRS. KELLER

Welcome to Success! This course is designed to introduce you to Shakespearean acting and the responsibilities of technical production. **Everyone in this class will have an opportunity to perform in this year's production of** *A Midsummer Night's Dream* . Auditions, Interviews, and Rehearsals will take place during class time, with the exception of one weekend, and two Thursday afternoons. During Production Week, you will need to make yourself available every evening from 5:30-8:30. The production dates for *Midsummer* are April ⬛⬛ and ⬛ with possible matinees for invited schools. In the Fall Semester, the focus will be on *Angel Street*. The dates for that are December 2,3, and 4; everyone in this class will have a production/technical position for that play. You are expected to make yourself available during production week. This is going to be an exciting year in production for Westwood with yourselves as the primary company!

FIRST ПINE WEEKS

Week One: Getting to know you!! Procedures and Routines.

Week Two: Fundamentals of Design and Theatre Management
                Duties and Responsibilities of Teams

Week Three: Production Crews established.
                  Begin Read Thru
Week Four: Begin Production Meetings

Midsummer
april 6, 7ᵗ, 8ᵗʰ

Week Five: Begin Design ; put in orders as needed.
Week Six: Design
Week Seven: Design; Construction Begins
Week Eight: Construction (cont)
Week Nine: Construction (cont).
Week Ten: Construction (cont). End of Grading Period. (October 22)

Figure 5.2.   Sample Syllabus

easy to follow, with appropriate use of boldface. It's also clearly written for the student.

• *Step Four: Revising for Consistency of Voice*

Prefab syllabi are notorious for their hodgepodge approach to voice. Sometimes, for example, the syllabus author will use second person (*you*). In other instances, it's third person (*students*) or first person plural (*we/our*).

So many people have worked on these syllabi that any sense of cohesion is completely lost. It's up to you to ensure that what's handed down from the district makes sense. Thus, any prefab comments should be refreshed.

To begin building the sense of the class *as a class*, consider using first person plural (*we/our*) as much as possible. It's personal as well as building on the concept of the class as an entity. Figure 5.3 shows a revision from multiple

Pre-Fab	Revised
As students progress from one course to the next, increases should occur in the complexity of materials and tasks and in the students' independence in the application of skills and strategies. *You will receive a list of "hot words" to use in your papers, which you will keep in this section of your notebook.*	As we move from one course to the next, the complexity of what you read and do will increase. Also, we'll be working on independent learning skills. Every week, we'll have a list of "hot words" to use in assignments. It's a good idea to keep them in the Vocab section of your notebook!

Figure 5.3.   Wording Syllabus in One Voice

voices to a singular voice from different points in a syllabus. Consider which of the two conveys a stronger sense of *class*. The overuse of second person (you/your) comes across as commanding, and the use of third person (*students*) completely depersonalizes the document. One voice will subtly reinforce the concept of one class.

Phase Two: A Living, Breathing Document

Okay, you've done all that you can with what you've been given. The formatting, font, and voice are consistent. It actually looks like something. Could you stop here and just use the general info and topics? Sure. You could. However, by doing so, you'll miss out on the one opportunity you have to be totally creative-genius with it: creating a course outline.

COURSE OUTLINE

A course outline differs from the syllabus in that it resembles a calendar of events, assignments, and goals. Your prefab syllabus might come with a quarterly or semester play-by-play, and a revision of this information will help you spot opportunities to recalibrate or maneuver within its curricular confines.

*In order for teachers to find the passion you had, they must be able to contend
with the restrictions and limitations of the system.* ~ *Daniel*

• *Step One: Make a List*

After you've formatted and so on, you'll want to make a list of what
the district/school expects of your classes. What specific assignments are
required and/or expected in each particular nine weeks? For example, our
hypothetical syllabus might require a student research project in the first nine
weeks. Okay! That goes on your list.

You'll also have to consult the scope and sequence (S/S) for your course
and grade level, which may have additional expectations. If you don't know
what that is or where to get it, you can consult an administrator, but you might
want to take a look at your district website first. Sometimes, they're on the site.

Your S/S may have *annual* objectives (what the district wants you to do
within the academic year), or it may have *semester/quarterly* objectives. The
quarterly objectives might resemble Figure 5.4.

My County Public Schools English II Scope and Sequence

Course: English II   Grade: 10   Course Code: 1234566   Q: 2

Strand: Reading Process

Standard: Vocabulary Development:

The student uses multiple strategies to develop grade-appropriate
vocabulary.

Content/Concepts Objectives
The student will:

ENV 12345.1: *use context clues to decipher unknown vocabulary.*

ENV 12345.2: *consistently apply real-world activities to understand
new vocabulary.*

Figure 5.4.   Sample Objectives in Scope and Sequence

While maybe not quite as tangible as the requirements on your prefab syllabus, the S/S still contains *implied* requirements. For example, in Figure 5.4, the implication is that you will, at some point in the second nine weeks (Q: 2) teach the use of context clues for vocabulary to meet the standard for vocabulary development, which falls under the umbrella of Reading Process. Look for and include those *student will* statements.

This vital information helps you determine *where* a particular lesson will work most effectively in a specific quarter, and now is the time to consider *where* in constructing your course outline. A little detective work and list-making will help you come up with a workable list.

With your revised syllabus and the district scope and sequence in front of you, start listing:

First Nine Weeks List
From the syllabus:

Two test dates TBA, sometime during Week Two
Research essay (options: argument <u>or</u> expository on tension developed in another country)
8 Reading selections (order of reading optional)
Teach vocabulary of 50+ terms
Oral Presentation of research project

From Scope and Sequence: (*student will* statements)

use technology to make a presentation
write in a variety of expository forms
use technology for writing
analyze literary elements in fiction
create a synthesis argument using nonfiction

Create similar lists for each nine weeks to figure out the basics of what is expected in each quarter or semester. This is only the rough outline. From here, we can move onto molding it into something interesting and exigent.

Putting items together that seem to match will ease some of your anxiety. Notice that the research project and the synthesis argument of nonfiction could probably go together. Analyzing fiction with one of the reading selections is also a "match"!

From the list, determine what the "biggies" are—those requirements for students that will most likely take the most time.

For example, our lists indicate that a research paper and the presentation of that paper are two biggies for the first nine weeks. Presentations are great, but they eat up a huge amount of classroom time. Thus, our choice of *when* to do these presentations will be critical to our sanity (if the choice is offered). Course outlines help us offset potential issues with timing before we even begin.

- *Step Two: Determining the Overarching Question or Theme for the Year (Or: If your curriculum has a prefab theme, add it in here! ~ Stacey)*

Brainstorming the question:
After determining what students are expected to do in each term, review the required readings/chapters. What seems to stand out amongst all of these selections? To what question do all of these selections seem to respond?

Here's a list of some required readings from a prefab syllabus for English I:

"Where Have You Gone, Charming Billy?" by Tim O'Brien
"No News from Auschwitz" by A. M. Rosenthal
Night by Elie Wiesel
"The Butterfly," by Pavel Friedmann
Into Thin Air (excerpt) by Jon Krakauer
"R.M.S. *Titanic*" by Hanson W. Baldwin

Out of these six choices, four have to do with the Holocaust or war, and two deal with disasters. The immediate response might be to go with one of those themes. However, if you really want to pull things together, you're going to have to think *bigger* and, potentially, less depressingly.

For a literature course, all of these selections could point to either choices humanity makes/has made or the consequences of those choices. The case for *Into Thin Air* is the weakest in application of choices because it's about the Mt. Everest disaster. However, one could bring in the choices made in reaction to this disaster.

Thus, "Choices" seems to be a good working theme. Make the most of your theme. It is the one wisp of creativity you have to make this syllabus truly yours. As you review all of the requirements, see what umbrella all of your required stuff might fit under.

Granted, making the connections to choices will need some tweaking, but it is a tangible connection—a thread that will be woven throughout the entire nine weeks and possibly the school year. Moreover, the concept of choices is something that relates to teens, and they will enjoy arguing this sort of topic. We're on our way!

Creating the question:
We have a topic for a theme, but we also need a question. The use of a question is multipurpose: it helps students think, provides fodder for discussion, establishes a purpose for the work, and sets a tone. Moreover it rein-

forces that you possess an intellectual curiosity. Again, *you* are the model for critical thinking, the core of which is questioning. What better way to introduce the concept than on your guiding document?

It's a lot easier for the student to remain attentive in class if there's a clear agenda. Without any sense of direction, through either a theme or overarching question, I often found myself more concerned with advancing my imagination than applying myself towards the task at hand.

Again, it's a simple a premise that some teachers had and others didn't. Yet it serves as another strong connection in determining which teachers I still remember and, ultimately, which ones had the most impact on my education and my life. ~ Daniel

Creating an overarching question that addresses the theme is your goal. Think in global terms, such as "humanity" or "society." These concepts are general enough to avoid some of the micro-issues teenagers seem to revel in. Here are some potential ideas, based on Choices:

• What drives us, as humans, to make choices?
• What compels me to make the choices I do?
• What compels others to make the choices they do?

All of these questions would work, and more than likely, you can pull from each of them throughout the year. They are open-ended and ripe for argument! Consider working from the biggest idea as the overarching question because you can always move conceptually smaller in a selected unit. So, our biggest idea/question is, "What drives us, as humans, to make choices?"

• *Step Three: Using the Question to Drive the Course*

What works well with this sort of question is that adolescents will naturally lean towards argument to respond—they have an opinion. Their initial opinion might be that peer pressure or money drives people to make choices, whether good or bad. Fine. As they read each and every selection from the list, they will want to be on the lookout for validation or refutation of their initial opinions.

More importantly though, this question will give them a *reason* to read or understand—if only to prove that their opinions are right. Hence, the vision of a class of students who think, argue, and prove is well on its way, and you haven't even started!

I remember loving this! On the first day of a new unit, we would discuss "What is Beauty?" or "What is Evil?" All to answer the overarching question: "What makes us human?"

I loved hearing and digesting what everyone had to say and what their per-
spectives were. This is where I began to love literature because of the discus-
sions and what everyone brought to the table. ~ Stacey

• *Step Four: Creating the Outline Template*

The outline is the living part of the syllabus. It is flexible, but it's also
very strong. To ensure that we meet all expectations and stay true to our vision and question, we're going to create a master template for the class and
course, based on the academic calendar and any known dates/events for each
quarter. These are the things we have to work the curriculum "around," and
they impact your choice for units.

(*Advice before beginning this step:* Work on the outline in stages. Don't try
to do it all at once. Consider working on one quarter at a time.)

Some events are obvious to include (teacher workdays, for example), but
you'll also want to include any district or school-wide testing dates. The more
specific you can be, the better off you are! Out of forty-five teaching days
in the first nine weeks, you may find that you actually only have thirty-three
teaching days. Whew! Your template might look like this *before you even*
add in any curriculum:

First Nine Weeks
    Week Six:
        Holiday and Teacher Workday 9/29 and 9/30
        SATs 10/1
    Week Seven:
        Half-Day Friday 10/7
    Week Eight:
        PSAT 10/13–10/16

Out of these three weeks, or fifteen days, you have eleven full instructional
days, possibly twelve. Don't make the mistake of thinking the PSAT only impacts tenth graders. This test impacts all of the other grades, too. The seniors
may be taken out for separate activities; the juniors and freshmen probably
won't be changing classes (to avoid the distraction of the bell). You might
also be asked to administer the test. Thus, this test does impact your day one
way or another.

• *Step Five: Inputting the Curriculum*

Now, grab your list. Locate the biggies on your course outline as strategically as possible. In *what week*, or in *what order*, will these larger assign-

ments work most effectively? What other required assignments seem to build up to those bigger assignments, thus emphasizing cohesive *purpose*?

Granted, a presentation is best accomplished after the paper is written, so putting those biggie due dates back-to-back (paper due, then presentation), allotting for two days (or one block) of presentation time makes sense.

Sometimes, it's helpful to work *backwards* from a biggie, identifying how to build up to it. For example, if you have a test on plate tectonics, what information/assignments need to be done *prior* to this test? How should you work *around* workdays, holidays, and test days to get to the biggie? This is another way to make the outline a living document for the students.

It's also helpful to include some days in which the assignment is take-it-or-leave-it (FYI only). That way, you'll have some breathing room for the inevitable impromptu assignments that will come from administration or the district, such as a sudden school-wide test question, reading, or unexpected writing prompt.

Planning ahead for any interruptive sort of assignments from the powers above and emphasizing the need for flexibility on the student's part will help involve him/her in the process. This approach underscores your transparent approach and enhances your rapport—you are in this together as a class as *we*.

• *Final Step: What to Do with the Completed Document*

Congratulations! You're the proud parent of a personalized, prefabricated syllabus and course outline! This rather daunting document serves to please your district *and* you (hopefully). However, it's unwieldy and cumbersome for students. Unless otherwise specified by your administration, consider the following suggestions:

• Post the entire syllabus on your classroom website with the option for download and printing.
• Create a class set (forty copies) of all pages with the exception of the course outline. Use the class set only for overview at the beginning of the year and keep them handy for reference as needed. (Rationale: saves paper.)
• Create copies of the course outline for every student—*this is the part of the document that they need to keep and work with*. Consider using colored paper for this outline for quick retrieval.

Hopefully, by the time you've completed your document, you're left with a sense of excitement for the upcoming year. Or, at the very least, you're a little bit excited about some of your upcoming discussions/projects.

CREATING SYLLABI AND COURSE OUTLINES

If you have the ability to revise or create your own syllabi (lucky you!), you'll still want to consider undertaking this task when you are relaxed and not under duress.

For tackling the creation of the syllabus, teachers need to remember: be concise. While there is a plethora of important information that needs to be included in this almighty packet—why say something in ten pages if it can be done in five? A list of dates and times is naturally long, so the real focus is on the precise, direct points of the course. ~ Crystal

Courses You've Taught Before and Are Teaching Again

For these courses, reviewing your lesson plan notes and student evaluations from the previous terms will help you determine what went exceptionally well (your "keeper" assignments), what you may want to improve upon, and what projects/assignments need to be removed or relocated. Most districts expect you to submit your lesson plan books for record-keeping. Thus, you'll want to determine a method for keeping copies of these crucial notes for yourself.

Providing your new class with relevant feedback from the former class is also an option for a repeat course. For example, if your students really liked a certain project, include their comments about it on the syllabus.

I really liked your syllabus because it had comments from the students the previous year. I felt that I could trust them and you just from that piece of paper. ~ Stacey

I loved the references that reflected on previous courses. Students need to see that teachers care where they have been so that they can help get to new heights! I always felt that way in your classes. Each one built upon the last, and I knew exactly what was going to take place. Since you were informed, I was informed. I was prepared. The confidence you had in your plan set me up to succeed. Those are priceless tools and starting the class with those tools is essential! ~ Crystal

The trust Stacey refers to is an invaluable asset to increasing student willingness to learn as well as discipline. Additionally, if this document can set a student up to succeed, as Crystal perceived it, then these syllabi, which we might be cursing inwardly, speak louder than we may realize.

Also, take a few moments to review any changes to the district scope and sequence/syllabi. It's usually clearer if you do so from a hard copy. Of course, these types of documents are still subject to change even after the school year begins, but *editing* is easier than creating.

Consider things you might have learned, gleaned, or stolen from other instructors during the previous school year. For example, you might find a fellow teacher has a great idea for presenting the Civil War. Use his or her ideas in the revised course outline.

Because you are under no pressure or deadline, your wherewithal to pull all of this together will be more effective. The outcome is a far more creative, structured, and reflective syllabus/course outline. Moreover, with the attention to detail, the curriculum will not only meet district and state expectations, it will probably exceed them.

The comfort of using a tried-and-true syllabus is quite appealing. Of course, it would be so nice to just switch out that academic year, change the dates, and move on. However, every year brings you the chance to start over and improve. Teaching is one of the few careers that possess the quality of renewal.

At other jobs, you're able to start anew each January 1, but, you're (usually) working with the same staff, same clientele, etc. With teaching, you have brand-new personalities filtering in and out each year. There's no way that two years/ two classes/two semesters even will be the same.

Why not use last year as a blueprint of what to fix for this year? Embracing the opportunity of renewal for teachers gives the incoming students a fresh start themselves. ~ Christina

You don't want your kids at just the *state* level of expectations; you want them at *your* level of expectation. The only way to achieve this goal is to exceed that level yourself, every year, with every course, whether repeated or new.

The best teacher to learn from is the one who is capable of learning. Both teaching and teacher should be a work in progress, because wherever there's room for growth, there is room for opportunity. ~ Daniel

Creating a Syllabus for a Course You've Never Taught

There's something incredibly exciting about teaching a new course and having the permission to choose the path of curriculum. It's like shopping or putting a team together—you can pick and choose what may or may not work with your school's students. Additionally, you have the creative license to go a "mile deep" as opposed to a "mile long" in your approach.

You'll want to determine if there is a specific text you're required to use. This will be the most limiting factor, so it's your first stop. You'll also want to take a look at your department's library of supplemental texts for possibilities. Enjoy the freedom of creating your own course. Make it rich, fertile ground for critical thinkers to thrive upon.

CLASS PLANNER/JOURNAL ENTRIES

After you've created your course outline, you'll also want to input significant dates in an academic planner or journal. Whether you opt for a digital weekly/monthly planner, an app for your phone, or a hard copy (available at most office supply stores), you'll experience a sense of accomplishment by putting in reminders for the school year before it begins. This planner will tell a story that you'll use along the way as well as for next year's planning.

Testing dates, holidays, half days, breaks, and administrative due dates should be input first. General notes work best on the monthly view or page. Then, you'll want to give yourself "reminder" notes or alarms. For example, one week before grades are due, you might put in a reminder: *Grades Due Next Week*.

Other items to consider incorporating are annual community events, such as parades, festivals, and county fairs. You'll want to know when homecoming, prom, extracurricular competitions, and senior activities are. If nothing else, you can help students (who may be heavily involved in these events) understand how to plan and organize around these events, rather than "catching up" afterwards. If you don't know the specific dates, use last year's dates as a guideline.

It may sound redundant to consider all of this information on both an outline and in a planner, but once you're in the flow of the school year, the last thing you want is to be surprised that a due date or half day has arrived so soon. And though you may have a very sharp memory by all accounts, you simply can't remember everything. Using a planner and including overarching dates ahead of time (with relevant reminders), you are living Aristotle's claim that "Well begun is half done."

I see so many of my peers ground down to a pulp before school even starts because they're trying to cram all of this planning into a week or two. The excitement to bring the kids on board is lost! Spacing the planning out is a fantastic idea—do it on your own time before you even have to worry about it!

The obvious problem is if you don't know what you'll be teaching. Unfortunately, more and more teachers are being moved around without warning, sometimes teaching a different grade or subject than planned. The impact on students is greater than administrators realize. ~ AnnMarie

This planning time is productive, creative, and stress free. There simply isn't time to do this sort of planning at the start of school, as you'll see in later chapters. At this time of year, before the great rush, you will be able to do what you were taught in numerous education courses: develop curriculum tailored to students' needs.

All in all, you can expect to spend approximately two to three hours revamping a repeat course and two to three days working on a new course. However, printing out those master syllabi and course outlines will really, really feel good. You are halfway there!

Chapter Six

Birds, Bees, Procedures, and Discipline

Another component that works well when tackled in the summer is the development of your procedures and discipline plan. As a new educator, you may think you have miles to go before you teach; however, you are closer than you think. Veteran teachers, you'll want to pull any relevant handouts that pertain to classroom management or discipline for comparative review with this chapter.

Thus far, you've visualized your ideal class, and you have a good idea of how you're conveying your teacher persona (or intend to). Additionally, you've started or completed your welcome calls and course planning. Good!

Now, you're going to determine a concrete, tangible way to present *what* you want your students to do and *how*. The best way to do that is to think in terms of what you already know: by observing or recalling how adults handle class experiences.

Seminars, classes, and in-services are especially intriguing to analyze from the perspective of what adult teacher-participants do and how they behave. For all intents and purposes, they are the *students*, and the speaker-presenter is the *teacher*.

Moreover, these classes automatically seem to mesh into a productive, authentic learning experience (an ideal class?). We've talked a lot about what the teacher's responsibilities are, but what are these adult-students doing or not doing that seems "okay" as it pertains to logistics and behavior?

For example, adults talk during seminars. Oh, they'll do it quietly, but they will lean over to their neighbors from time to time, generally providing on-topic commentary or possibly unwarranted criticism.

They'll get up to go the bathroom, discreetly leaving and returning. They eat and drink, replenishing themselves with coffee and donuts *a bene placito*.

They text, doodle, surf, and, for the most part, participate in what's expected without much ado.

They do nothing to "bug" the presenter or their fellow participants or to stop the flow of information. The presenter does not have to delve into any explanations that are *givens*. It's a *given* that you can get up and get something if need be. It's a *given* that you can quietly talk to your neighbor.

Unfortunately, it's the students' lack of understanding those *givens* that drives teachers to the brink, which in turn compounds student misbehavior. If you get your procedural ducks in a row, however, your need for discipline will greatly decrease. They are two different things that work *together* to create a whole experience.

The givens are the *procedures* we must explicitly teach and consistently maintain with students. And while we may think the givens are no-brainer-face-palm-obvious, adolescents just don't have them yet. They really, really don't understand these givens. *Bemoaning that fact won't change it.* By creating general procedures that address these givens, you will catch most of the issues that lead to grey hair and/or lack thereof.

We will address the exercise of disciplining behavior a bit later, but for now, try to hold to the theory that students need to be taught what to do, when to do it, and how to do it, for your class. It doesn't matter whether they are seniors or freshmen, you will approach the conception of your general procedures and rule(s) as though these students have never set foot in civilized society.

> *The teachers who seem to consistently work well with their classes are the ones who approach issues logically and with the clear intent of modeling proper behavior—all with the underlying theme of respect.*
>
> *And respect, unlike the common idiom, is not something you should have to earn. At the high school level, not a ton of kids understand how to earn it. Respect must be modeled, whether students deserve it or not, which completely goes against the norm—both theirs and ours. But in some cases, where else are they supposed to see it work? ~ AnnMarie*

The two parts of the givens, procedures and a rule(s), are a concept to which this author gratefully attributes to Harry and Rosemary Wong's *The First Days of School: How to Be an Effective Teacher*. The following strategies are an adaptation of their distinction between the two.

PROCEDURES (THE BIRDS)

Procedures are those actions that have anything to do with what the student or teacher does during the course of the class. They are grounded in that "doing" principle. They are the *what* of the class.

From *what* the teacher does to quiet the class, to *what* students do to submit their homework, procedures are noninterpretive and objective. They are cemented in stone and not subject to argument—not because they are higher laws, but because they are logical, practical, and, simply, make sense.

Categorizing Procedures

First, you'll want to categorize them. Obviously, you may come up with more effective and/or relevant ones, depending on your course. For example, an AP class might have stricter or more flexible procedures for paper submissions than a remedial reading course. Some general categories for any course might be:

General Doing Stuff Procedures
Group Procedures
Class Discussion Procedures
Presentation Procedures
Half-Day Procedures
Grading/Return of Papers Procedure
Weekly Grade and Printout Procedures
After-School/Emergency Procedures

It's helpful to create separate documents for General, Group, and Presentation procedures. That way, you'll have them available as handouts for students prior to their immediate use. You'll only need to hand out the General Procedures that first week, but defining all categories for yourself (at your leisure) will result in a stronger overall management plan.

Brainstorming an Effective Procedure

After you've categorized, you'll want to create the most important group: *General Doing Stuff.* Ask yourself: "What things do students do that drive me kooky-crazy?"

Keep in mind that we're not discussing how they behave *when* they're doing something. You want to identify specifically *what* it is that they do. You might write it out like this:

It drives me crazy when . . .
   students sharpen their pencils at the worst
      possible times.

The procedure for sharpening pencils in a class is a given to adults in our hypothetical seminar: one doesn't sharpen a pencil while someone else is talking. One does so before the presentation or during an activity or break. Easy enough, right?

However, high school students have a strange, random compulsion to go up to the pencil sharpener at the worst possible time: when the teacher is *talking*. Just the thought of that whirrr-whirrr-whirrr is enough to make you grind your teeth, and when this No. 2 connoisseur has a penchant for that perfectly sharpened fine-tip, this process will continue until lead meets eraser.

This distraction inevitably leads to bickering, distraction, or comments . . . something. Consider, then, rewording your "what drives me crazy" thinking into this procedure:

Sharpen pencils when it is least distracting.

Putting the procedure in positive terms helps because students then understand that the action is sanctioned. However, *when* to do that action involves some discretion. The message you send to students will be "I am going to trust your judgment."

As you brainstorm your procedures, you'll want to focus in on these qualities:

- It's something students *do* that you are unwilling to "let go" or "let slip by."
- It has a clear and logical justification.
- It has been reduced down to the simplest form.
- It's phrased positively.

All the books tell us to do this, but you're explaining how and why, and that's helpful. ~ Stacey

Temptation through the phrasing can often be the source and solution to some management issues. The temptation to push the big red button is stronger when the message is "Do Not Push This Big Red Button!"
However, if the message is "Consider circumstances before pushing big red button," the temptation is a lot weaker. ~ Daniel

Most Important Procedure

Something that drives any teacher crazy is trying to get students to be quiet and listen to instructions. The signal for *Gaining the Attention of the Class* is really the most crucial. In our adult class, above, how do the adult-students know when *not* to talk or when to *stop* talking? Usually, the presenter simply says, "Good Morning" (that does the trick for the first part of the session). All of our teacher-students dutifully turn their attention to the presenter.

After a break, usually an "Okay, it's about that time, so let's go back to . . ." or "Now that everyone's back, let's get started!" seems to work.

All verbal. Plus, presenters have the microphone advantage. All teacher-students stop what they're doing and move to their seats or pay attention.

While a verbal cue may work for teachers of high schoolers during the honeymoon phase (those first days of school), *it doesn't work after the first day or so.* You must create an attention-getting procedure that you find natural to do that is not verbal.

My "Hand" procedure emerged early during my education coursework. I was a guest teacher, working with a volunteer in the district. The class was expected to discuss a short story, and they had just come back from lunch. Of course, they were wired and talkative.

I was on my own because my overseeing teacher stepped outside (as per the course requirement). I tried the verbal thing, "Okay, everyone!" to no avail. I didn't want to shout at them or speak loudly. So, I found myself holding up my hand as if I had a question.

Their reaction was interesting! They slowly stopped talking long enough for me to ask a question towards the actual lesson. *Eureka!* So, I used it again and again along the way through my practicum—it worked every time.

Another reason I decided to use this procedure was because in my classroom observations, I would hear teachers yelling, which hurt my ears. Thus, the quietness of the Hand satisfied me. I also observed teachers doing the light-switch thing. Well, that bothered my eyes. Again, the Hand won out.

> *"The Hand" was a staple of all three years I spent under Mrs. K. I can personally affirm its effectiveness because many times I chose to test her patience. I wasn't always the most obedient of her students (I was the impetus and original winner of the Darth Keller Award for Evil, after all).*
>
> *However, I can't recall ever trying the might of "The Hand." Even I recognized that such a simple gesture represented a line that should not be crossed. What I find more interesting is that I remember coming to that conclusion intuitively. Mrs. K would go on to explain and confirm its purpose, but its initial usage alone was enough for me to grasp its nature. ~ Daniel*

We will discuss the particulars of the execution of this procedure, but for now, think about what you can do that is simple, nonverbal, and natural for you.

Procedures List

A good solid number for general classroom procedures is around seven, given the human capacity for short-term memory. Remember, you're only creating procedures for *your* class and only *general* procedures, at first.

Here is a list that you may find helpful in alleviating the majority of the disruptive stress in the classroom, written with a student audience in mind.

This information could work as a separate handout (labeled "Procedures and Rules") or as part of a syllabus with that heading.

- *The Hand*: When I need the class's attention, I will raise my hand. When you see my hand up, please go to your seats and/or wait quietly for instructions.
- *Entering the Class*: When you enter the class, please get your folder from the box and read the board for instructions.
- *Ask Your Neighbor*: If you have a question about something, ask your neighbor first. If he/she does not have the answer, ask me.
- *Pencil Sharpening*: Sharpen pencils when it is least distracting to do so.
- *Tardy*: If you're tardy to class, please get your folder and take your seat. I'll come to you as soon as I'm able to find out what happened and retrieve your tardy slip.
- *Bathroom*: If you need to use the restroom, please use the hall pass located next to the projector and quietly leave the class.
- *End of Class*: Please place folders in the class box and remain in your seat or at your seat until the bell rings.
- *Leaving the Classroom*: If you need to leave the classroom for any reason (nurse, locker, etc.), please make your request after the class has been given instructions and is working.

Why the Procedures Work

While all of the procedures are recommended, one procedure that might be standing out to you is the "Ask Your Neighbor" procedure. It raises eyebrows because it seems to advocate talking while the teacher is talking. Why, yes, it does! However, the discussion is *on-task* and nondisruptive. Students talking, *even when the teacher is talking*, helps the class move along more smoothly.

Veteran teachers can attest to the following scenario. New teachers, you'll want to avoid this tragicomedy!

"What Page, Huh?"
A play in 180 Acts

TEACHER: Okay, everybody! Let's turn to page 432 in the workbook.

STUDENTS 1, 4, and 17: (*over the din of pages rippling violently*) What page, Ms./Mr.? Did you say 422?

STUDENT 2: (*yelling*) PAGE 432!

TEACHER: (*at the same time*) Page 432. Student Two, please don't—

STUDENT 10: (*loudly*) Which book?

STUDENT 2: What?

TEACHER: Your workbook. It's not necessary to yell.

STUDENT 8: Page 432?

STUDENT 2: I'm just trying to help!

TEACHER: Yes, I realize . . . It's written right here, you see? (*somewhat indignantly points to relevant spot on the overhead or board*)

STUDENTS flip through pages with great fervor as if their very lives depended on getting to that page.

TEACHER: Okay, take a look at—

STUDENT 22: Wait! I'm not there yet!

STUDENT 24: Hang on!

TEACHER: (*either sarcastically sweet or sardonically stoic*) Is everyone ready now?

It doesn't matter if you write the page number on the board, the overhead, or sticky-note it your forehead; someone is going to ask for a repeat. The lesson will go off course before it even begins!

So, consider a procedure that mimics the hypothetical class. We, the adults, ask the person next to us, very quietly, "What page did she say?"

Emphasize to students that the procedures you implement are based on your experiences with adult courses. This emphasis comes with a Catch-22 included because what do teenagers generally desire the most? To be treated like adults! (Never *state* this generalization, however. Let them *infer*, based on your comparisons and explanations. They'll feel good about themselves.)

However, they're usually not taught *how* to do anything like an adult. Rather, the expectations would be set, period. That's not enough, frankly. Thus, any time the student has a question, about anything, the first course of action is to ask a neighbor (the only exception being a test or exam).

Do students ever take advantage of this? Usually not. However, that would move them into "rule" territory, which is a bit different than the procedures.

I could've used a procedure like this in more of my classes. There were many times where my imagination would wander, and I'd miss some vital information regarding the lesson. These scenarios could have been easily rectified had I been permitted to simply consult a nearby student.

However, many of the classes that were conducive to my waning attention span were also run by those who fiercely opposed communication during those moments. On many occasions, I found myself intellectually removed from the immediate lesson because I felt unable to confirm its direction due to fear of earning the ire of the teacher. The result not only made me very uncomfortable but made my lessons more difficult than they needed to be. ~ Daniel

Another effective procedure is the Tardy Procedure. As adults, we know that if we're late to an event, our goal is to slink in as quietly as possible and sit down. However, high school students have a tendency to stroll in and take that opportunity to tell the instructor the whole long, drawn-out story about why they're late, grabbing the entire room's attention and routing everyone off course.

This very common interruption is definitely not desirable. Once you start the class, you'll want to keep the flow going. Thus, your procedure for "being late" can be that students slink in as quietly as possible, lay the tardy slip on the desk, and get in the groove with everybody else.

Because the tardy slip and/or hall pass (usually an obnoxiously conspicuous neon hue) will be on the student's desk, you'll have a visual reminder that the student was late, and at a moment of *your* choosing, you will listen to the whole story.

Notice that all of these procedures seem so logical. However, students will need to practice and rehearse, and you will need to remind them over and over and over again.

One of your goals is to not yell at them for forgetting the procedure, no matter how many times they have managed to forget. You can, instead, remind them by leaning over and conspiratorially whispering, "What should you do? What's the procedure for when you're tardy?"

This strategy will give the student the opportunity to redeem him/herself, and it will give you an opportunity to smile and say, "Thanks."

Prepare yourself to do this reminder thing for at least a semester, if not well into the third quarter. We'll address some strategies for keeping your cool with reminders a bit later.

The important thing is to not lose the *graciousness* of the procedures by stressing that gratitude for their implementation. Underneath the reminders is the belief that students really do want procedures and organization. However, *how* they behave is a different component.

THE RULE (THE BEES)

I really admire teachers who can maintain their calm. I have seen a teacher go nose-to-nose with a student in a screaming match. It actually dragged more students into the dispute, so then there were multiple students screaming at the teacher. No one wins. And the teacher lost complete control of the classroom. ~ Crystal

If procedures are the *what* of your classroom management, then the rule(s) you create is the *how* of your discipline plan. One nice aspect of a school's code of conduct policy is that the really rough behavior (drugs, fighting, smoking) is covered. If this occurs in your classroom, you *already* know what needs to be done. These are no-brainers for teachers.

It's the other stuff under the behavior category, those in-between behaviors, that will drive you to distraction. You already know, or probably have a very good idea, of how you'd react to two kids beating each other up. But, how do you respond to horseplay?

Crafting a well-developed rule that encompasses pretty much every possible behavioral issue is tricky. It should be flexible and general enough to work in any situation, but specific, concise, and memorable. For high schoolers, consider the use of one rule:

Respect your teacher, your classmates, and your classroom at all times.

This rule, printed out in large letters, should hang in a visible spot in the classroom.

Why Only One Rule for High Schoolers?

One advantage of this one-rule policy is that you'll never feel oppressed by it. For example, you make a rule that states, "No Food or Drinks." Then, if *you* ever want to have something to drink, or if the class wants/deserves to have a party, you're stuck with it. If you don't follow the rule, then you lose your credibility with the class.

Moreover, the flexibility of one rule allows for an equally flexible response to the breaking of it. We'll discuss how to execute this response in a later chapter, so for now, we'll work on the planning of it.

Figure 6.1 presents a *non-example* Discipline Plan that may prove helpful. It's a compilation of what you'll see on most teachers' Discipline Plans. It adheres to the old-school method of C.Y.A. However, it will be ineffective with adolescents.

First, the teacher has presented too many rules and mixed them up with procedures. All of these rules, really, would fall under the category of respect. Including each of them will set you up for a court battle with students. These Legal Lemurs (for lack of a better term) will loophole you to death.

"Well, the rules don't sayyyyyyy that I can't rap during class . . ."

Indeed, there is a loophole for this action in numbers 3–6, and as much as you'd like to think your use of *et cetera* covers you, it doesn't. When used in a list of very specific items, *etc.* conveys the sense that the writer just got tired of writing.

Classroom Rules

A. Classroom Rules are posted in the classroom. Let's quickly review what each rule means.

> Why state the obvious? Why *write* what you're going to do?

1. Respect the teacher and classmates. (You respect the teacher when you do what you're told, don't talk back, do not touch any personal property without permission, and follow all classroom rules and procedures. You respect your classmates when you follow classroom rules and procedures.)

> Including specific situations on the plan dilutes the impact of the rule.

2. Follow directions. (This means that you do whatever the teacher tells you to do without complaining or arguing about it. Example: return books, go back to seat, copy from board, stop talking, etc.)

> From a student's perspective, how does this make you feel?

3. Keep hands, feet, and objects to yourself. (This means you do not throw things, kick things, push people, hit people, etc.)

4. No swearing, teasing, or name calling. (You do not use obscene or vulgar language in the classroom for any reason. You do not make fun of or tease another classmate because of his color, race, language, religion, etc.)

> So, you want them in the *class* or in their *seats*?

5. Be in the classroom when the bell rings. (This means I want you in your seat as soon as you come into my classroom, and I want you to be on time.)

> Nos. 3-6 repeat the same idea: respect others.

6. Severe: No fighting, threats, or verbal abuse. (It is also extremely inappropriate to curse.)

Figure 6.1. Non-Example Discipline Plan: Rules

However, if the only rule was to respect classmates, teacher, classroom at all times, the student would not have much of a legal standing. Singing, in any form, at an *inopportune* time, would disrupt the workings of the class (thus, classmates) and qualifies as an infraction of disrespect. That said, rapping at a time when it would not disrupt anyone or anything would be okay! Again, the principle is the prudence of *when* to do the action (in this instance), not the action itself.

What's also intriguing about this non-example plan is that students would conveniently forget the first rule listed. However, if there is only *one* rule, they will have a harder time playing Legal Lemurs.

Also, consider the tone conveyed by these points on the non-example: You show respect to the teacher when you *passively obey*. Do whatever the teacher tells you to do without complaining or arguing about it. What type of persona seems to be conveyed here? Consider an identical memo coming to you from your principal (*Do whatever the principal tells you . . .*). Hmm.

Aren't we supposed to help these kids develop critical-thinking skills? How can they do that when respect is equated with power? Is that the message we want to send? This teacher uses language that cuts to this core: *I am the authority and power in this room, and don't you forget it.*

The Machiavellian approach may work as far as a stable work environment, but it will not further these students' thinking skills. It builds walls of resentment, not doorways of rapport.

The thinking behind the one rule and an emphasis on procedures is that you will *exude* authority without saying a word about it. You will hold the power: (1) explicitly, when it suits the needs of the class or coursework, and (2) implicitly, all the time.

TRUTH, NO CONSEQUENCES?

Consider leaving the consequences off of your student copy of the Discipline Plan. You can certainly provide your administrators with a lovely write-up and analysis of how you intend to respond to potential behavior problems. However, the students should only be faced with the rule.

Presenting specific consequences or a three-times warning + call home + send out is ridiculously tiring. Keeping track of the warnings, writing them on the board/overhead, and putting in check marks are disciplinary root canals. The worst part, really, is that including specific consequences gives teenagers fertile grounds for Legal Lemur Loophole opening arguments:

"You only warned me twice. I get another warning."

"Hey, you can't send me out! You didn't warn me first!"

You've got to hand it to those Lemurs when it comes to what their rights are. However, if you simply do not incorporate consequences, *you* have a wonderful loophole: your consequences can equitably correspond to the infraction. Figure 6.2 shows us why the consequence listing is far from a deterrent.

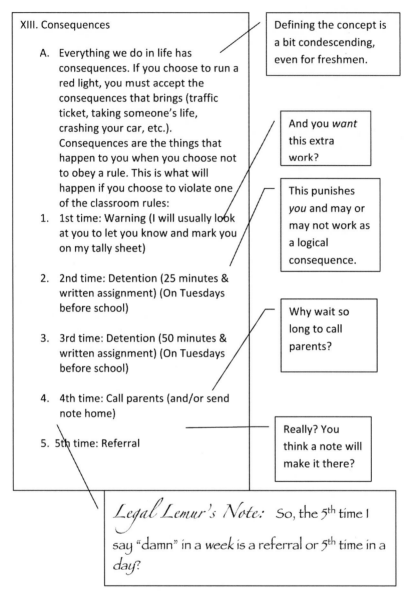

Figure 6.2. Non-Example Discipline Plan: Consequences

It's possible that your administration requires that you include consequences. Very well. Not much you can do there. However, if you have the flexibility to create your own, consider why you find it necessary to define the concepts of rules and consequences.

Perhaps it comes from so many years of having students not follow the rules? Nonetheless, *the threat of consequences simply does not deter behav-*

ior. (Especially when those consequences are more appropriate for elementary school.) Tally marks? Really?

Your smart-alecky student will be thinking: "OoooOOooo. You gonna look at me? You gonna gimme a tally? ooOOOOO."

Consider also that your house of consequential cards falls when a student *doesn't show up for detention* or shows up and refuses to do the assignment. Here, he or she has a little Legal Lemur Loophole for going back to the Warning Stage for something done *at* the Detention, which is a separate count, your Honor! Or they receive an in-school or out-of-school suspension for missing the detention, which again lands *you* more work because the student has missed your class. Thus, the legalities and follow-through of this plan collapse under their own weight.

(If you haven't seen it already, hopefully you see the value in having parents' e-mail addresses at this point?)

There's also a clarity issue as it pertains to the execution of these consequences. Are they per diem? If so, then the detentions do not work. Because if the student said "Damn" ten times between the time you made the tally marks and have the detention (next week?), then he/she is essentially getting away with the crime for a possible four days without recourse.

You can't provide recourse because the student hasn't worked through that step yet. These consequences are so much more frustrating for the teacher than the student, who already knows he's done something out of line. By the end, you're worn to a frazzle, and what has he learned from all of this? How to argue the *system*, not the behavior.

The temptation, again, lies within the definition, not only of their borders, but also in the consequences for stepping outside those parameters. It's more tempting to break the rules when a student knows the repercussions involved.

Creating a preset course of action won't prevent poor behavior. Rather, students may choose to act against the teacher so long as they find the known consequences to be acceptable. However, if the resulting disciplinary action is unknown, it not only allows the teacher some flexibility, but it also forces the student to consider that there are now risks to behaving out of turn.

Do they dare test the teacher when they don't know what will happen? Facing such a question can, and most likely will, curb many a destructive impulse. Not all of them, however, as an explorer of the forbidden will inevitably pop up on occasion. But it will certainly help handle those who face a simple inclination to do so, and they will be less determined to create problems. ~ Daniel

DETERMINING YOUR APPROACH TO CONSEQUENCES

Just because you haven't explicitly presented consequences to the students doesn't mean you won't *have* consequences. However, your goal is to think in terms of what makes sense, given the infraction. It's an exercise in "What would I do/say if a student . . .?"

Veteran teachers will want to work from those examples that maybe led to them losing their respective cools. New teachers, we've given you a scenario here, but you'll want to create some scenarios for yourself, based on what you saw in high school or observed in practicums. The principle, though, is: the consequence makes sense given *how* the rule was broken.

Scenario One: Potential Physical Altercation

Class has finished, and there are two minutes remaining before the bell rings. TEACHER is talking with some students near her desk, when she hears:

STUDENT A: *(Loudly to STUDENT B)* What the f—k is your problem?

STUDENT B: Oh, just shut up.

TEACHER: *(Moving in proximity, looking at both)* Ladies?

STUDENT A: *(Accusingly)* She just took my pen!

STUDENT B: No, I didn't, you b—!

TEACHER: *(Points to both when stating names, calmly and clearly, with a voice that brooks no argument)* A and B, please step out in the hall with me. *(Once in the hall, softly and clearly with resolve)* You have thirty seconds to resolve this situation respectfully. If you can't resolve it, then we are taking a walk to the dean. Go.

In this scenario, given the use of language and depth of anger, the teacher must immediately diffuse without contributing to the argument. That's the tricky part because our first instinct is to say, "Give her back her pen!" or "Why did you take her pen?" both of which *imply* guilt.

Another potential instinctual response is, "Did you take her pen?" which puts you on a side in the argument. You don't want that! You want these two students to learn how to deal with other people respectfully and resolve their own problems; thus, you must remain calm and objective.

Let's look at this same scenario, but see what happens when the attitude and tone are different.

Scenario Two: Verbal Altercation

Class has finished, and there are two minutes remaining before the bell rings. TEACHER is talking with some students near her desk, when she hears:

STUDENT A: *(Loudly to STUDENT B)* What the f—k is your problem?

STUDENT B: *(Laughing)* Shut up!

TEACHER: *(Moving in proximity, using an annoying singsong voice)* Please don't swear!

STUDENT A: *(In a baby voice)* She just took my pen!

STUDENT B: *(Mimicking the baby voice)* No, I didn't, you b—!

TEACHER: *(Slowly shaking head from side to side, makes eye contact with both, big sigh)* Such ugly words from such pretty faces.

TEACHER presents students with a kind of sad look, with a sort of smiley-frown on her face. Holds eye contact for about ten seconds, walks away with a big sigh.

Hopefully, you see why the teacher reacted in a completely different way. Scenario One focused on diffusing the threat of a physical altercation. Scenario Two focused on the issue of the use of profanity, all based on the teacher's understanding of the *context* of the behavior.

It's actually easier to deal with very serious issues, and students expect you to react. It's those more common, in-between, not-so-obvious areas, however, where teachers seem to falter or lose credibility.

The use of profanity is a topic that warrants further discussion because it is so prevalent in this age group. If we attempt to persuade ourselves that this language is anything but the norm in their conversations and culture, we are deceiving ourselves. It is analogous to not wanting your dog to bark. Dogs bark. Teenagers swear.

That doesn't mean that you're going to condone profanity. You certainly don't want it used in the classroom! However, depending on the circumstances, you will want to react as the situation merits.

Interestingly, an annoying singsong voice, which is a high-pitched saccharine (or for men, Pavarotti-esque) and presented in lispy rhythm, works wonders for easing the use of profanity in the classroom.

TEACHER: Pleaaaaase don't sweeeeeeaaar!

It is just enough to stop the behavior in a positive way and diffuse the moment. Also, the use of phrasing such as "Ugly words/pretty face" presents students with an incisive double-edged sword. Argue this point, and they have to own up to being not pretty/handsome (*Ching*! 1 point).

Moreover, after a month or so, you will seldom have to use that singsong voice. The students will probably pick it up and use it as needed towards their classmates. You may never have to say it again, reveling instead in the chorus of positive peer pressure.

Those methods really help you out with in-between profanity issues, but what to do when students swear at *you* has its own method.

Scenario Three: Profanity Aimed at the Teacher

Teacher has just handed back student tests and is preparing to review the results.

STUDENT: What the f—? How you gonna give me a D?

TEACHER: *(Moves to student, concerned look on the face)* Student? What's up?

STUDENT: Man, you gave me a D, and I know this ain't a D. This is bull—.

TEACHER: *(More concerned, calm, looks at paper)* Okay, let's make sure that I've graded you properly. I'm going to review the answers, and if you find that I've made a mistake, we'll definitely correct it!

STUDENT: *(Mumbles)* Effen bull—.

TEACHER: *(Whispers or mouths, again showing concern)* You okay?

TEACHER continues with review of test, often making eye contact with STUDENT for validation. After the class is busy working on something else, TEACHER goes back to STUDENT.

TEACHER: Everything okay?

STUDENT: Yeah, it's still BS though.

TEACHER: You know what, I'll take another look at it. I don't mind because it's made you very upset! *(emphasizes "very upset")*

STUDENT: 'kay.

TEACHER makes eye contact, using frowny-smile, waits.

STUDENT: Sorry for . . . you know.

TEACHER: *(Smiles)* Thanks.

Now, before you skeptics decide that the teacher should have commented on the profanity immediately, let's consider. The goal in this situation is not to *punish* the student for his behavior, which was undeniably disrespectful. The goal is to use context to teach the student to realize the degree of his or her behavior and self-regulate.

By listening to what the student is upset *about*, before jumping on the profanity wagon, you have an opportunity to validate him as a person before he's judged and sentenced. Moreover, he's been given an opportunity to show that he's aware his language is offensive, which is really what you want.

By waiting to assign consequences, the teacher allows the student to create his own. Isn't that the more powerful lesson? Isn't that something that will "stick" with the student? More than likely, that student will self-regulate again to that teacher, and that is respect.

Some may say that this is a power struggle, and the teacher loses because he or she gives in by agreeing to look at the paper again. That all depends on the goal, doesn't it?

Your goal for any students who use profanity in such a way is to have them self-evaluate and offer a sincere apology of their own accord. And this will happen. Your students will begin to "edit" themselves and even apologize for "almost" swearing. Or, they'll absent-mindedly swear and automatically say, "Sorry, Miss/Mr."

You *know* you are deserving of respect, and in this scenario, you will be the teacher who conveys that he/she deserves that respect.

"What if," suppose the skeptics, "the student *doesn't* apologize, huh? What are you going to do then, Ms. Fancypants?"

One fallback phrase pretty much covers any situation. In this instance, if the student doesn't apologize on his own, it might flow like this:

TEACHER: *(Calm, low, professional voice)* Student, let's talk outside for a second, okay?

STUDENT: *(Stubbornly, crossing arms)* No, and you can't make me, b—.

TEACHER: *(calm, but kind of sad and surprised)* Are you refusing to do as I ask?

STUDENT: That's right! Make me, b—.

TEACHER: *(Very low, so only the student can hear)* I've made a reasonable, polite request, and you've refused. That's your choice, and I'm going to follow up on this. I'll let you know at the end of class how we're going to handle this. *(Turns her back and walks away purposefully, but without anger.)*

Keep in mind that the isolated out-in-hall talk is really the best way to handle most issues. More than likely, you'll uncover the real reason for the student's behavior, which generally has nothing to do with you or the class. Plus, this outside talk allows for some bonding and building of rapport.

However, if necessary, the "student-only" whispering is the next best thing. Also, hold tightly to that "Are you refusing?" phrasing. It functions as a warning without being stated as such, and it gives the student a chance to make the right choice. Overall, the goal is to send this message: "I care about you, and I'm dead-serious about my rule."

Some of my teachers looked at discipline in an angry fashion instead of a means to understand what's going on. People don't act out because they're innately horrible people; they act out because there's an underlying issue.

If a student acts out, there's no way to resolve the situation properly until the initial issue is understood. In my experience as both student and teacher, anger is not the road to understanding, caring is. ~ Christina

So, what is the consequence? If the student refuses to cooperate, so that both of you can work out a solution, then e-mail the parent. You might write:

> Dear [Parent],
> [Student] seemed to be having a really tough day today. Please let me know because I'm worried about him.
>
> Kind regards,
>
> [Teacher]

Hopefully, the parent will provide some insight. You want the student to know that you *care* about whether or not he is having trouble—your dignity is not only intact, it is shining!

Many teachers approach discipline issues as action/punishment. Unfortunately, they fail to understand that it's not about punishing behaviors; it's about teaching proper behaviors. ~ AnnMarie

If you were using the old-school consequences method, then you would be "stuck" with following a program of consequences, none of which are suited for high school students.

Tally Marks? *Not for high school.*
Warnings? *Possibly, given the circumstances.*
Detentions? *Okay, but really more of a hassle for the teacher than the student.*

MY PRINCIPAL WANTS THE CONSEQUENCES ON THE PLAN FOR STUDENTS, TOO!

In the event that that your administrators want you to include the consequences on your *student copy* of the plan, you might consider the following wording:

> The consequences for breaking the rule will vary, depending on the extent to which you break it! Some examples of consequences might be, but are not limited to: e-mails to parents or phone calls home, apologizing to relevant parties, and/or a parent/teacher conference. I will treat each instance of the rule being broken fairly and logically.

Of course, for the *administrator copy*, you can emphasize the following:

1. My primary course of action for a student breaking the rule is to determine the *source* and context of the behavior. Why is the student breaking the rule and how?
2. From there, I will engage in mediation with the student on his/her behavior.
3. If mediation fails to elicit the desired behavior, I will contact the parent via e-mail or phone.
4. If the behavior persists as a pattern or seems to disrupt the class, I will call for a parent conference.
5. If the behavior is sufficiently aggressive or disruptive and endangers the class, I will call for the dean to remove the student.

These consequences should be quite pleasing to your administrator. You have a clear course of action for behavioral issues, and you have made a distinction between what can and should be handled by the teacher and when to call for assistance from the dean. As you give birth to your Procedures and Discipline plan, remember to:

- Make the distinction between Procedures and Rules.
- Formulate a nonverbal procedure for getting students' attention.
- Use procedures that make sense for your classroom.
- Limit the number of rules. One is preferable.
- Avoid listing specific consequences on your Discipline Plan, if possible.
- Think through some scenarios from your experience to help you create a logical approach to consequences.

By the time you're required to go to school, you'll not only be refreshed but excited about the upcoming school year. You'll be as prepared as you can be for what comes next: that *administrative-planning-research-classroom decorating- omg another in-service-faculty meeting-department meeting-vertical teaming-parallel discipline-scope and sequence following-syllabus adjusting* tarp of tension that constitutes pre-service days.

Chapter Seven

In the Eye of the
Pre-Service Storm

Yes, working during the summer is a crazy idea. Seriously, what is the perk that keeps many teachers in the profession? Summers off! That's what makes the crazy hair- pulling, sleepless school year worth it. But if we put in a few extra hours over a longer period of time, we actually end up with more time.
~ AnnMarie

If you haven't already taken the opportunity to visit your classroom, you'll want to think about doing so now. The inevitable required meetings and in-services of pre-service days leave educators with precious few hours to prepare their classrooms as they would like. Pre-service days, however, are truly vital for the working of the school as an institution and a team; everyone must be of one accord as it pertains to policy and procedure.

By following the strategies for preparatory work, these days can be primarily used as they are meant to be: for inspiration, insight, motivation, information, and, most importantly, that sense of "readiness."

PHYSICAL CLASSROOM AS PREEMPTIVE MANAGEMENT

Teachers not only need to own the material they present, but also own the physical environment in which they present. Physical surroundings, and how people move throughout them, directly affect students like me. ~ Crystal

Returning teachers should take a look at the physical layout of their classroom. Try to remember if there were any issues with sightlines or your ability to maneuver around and through desks/tables. Now is the time to fix it, if necessary.

For new teachers, you can use this time to consider the space for seating and arrangement of tables or desks. The peacefulness of creating your classroom without the distractions of meetings or other pre-service requirements cannot be overstated.

Focused Seating

There is an immediate accountability each student takes on by being in full view of his or her peers and instructor. ~ Crystal

Most instructors agree that the "rows upon rows" method of forming a classroom is obsolete. Consider that you can't really see every student in lengthy rows, thus increasing the probability of misbehavior. That's why subtly reinforced accountability is crucial.

I did love how your class was always set up "in the round"—that way we were always able to see the other students, and we had a clear shot of you when reading scripts, going over things, etc. It was very easy to communicate in that class. ~ Christina

Again, preemptively, you can begin to manage your class's behavior—one of the issues with classrooms is the lack of a sense of community. The ease of communication that Christina notes helps create that community, another means to enhance learning.

If your goal is a class of cooperative students, then a cooperative general setting will subtly reinforce that goal. As best you can, try to create a space that is no more than three seats deep, in roughly a U-shape. The goal is to give each student *a front seat*, facing center or forward. Figure 7.1 provides a generic possibility, using tables. (*Note:* Be aware of fire-code regulations for doors and exits.)

The classroom was a second home, set up as a semi-square shape around the sides and back wall of the room. We could all look at one another and turn to the center of our square to see Ms. Keller and the projector. ~ Crystal

Things get tricky if you have the idea that the blackboard or whiteboard must be the focus. Not necessarily. Crystal notes a subtle reinforcement that I hadn't considered before—when students *saw each other engaged* in the class, that engagement may have offset some potential issues. Thus, creating a seating arrangement in which the primary focus for the class is on *us* or *we* encourages community.

For the secondary or instructional focus, an overhead or opaque projector is much more transportable and flexible. Plus, the use of an overhead allows

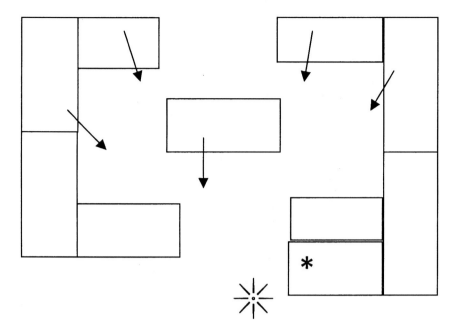

* Overhead/student folder boxes

❋ General focus of class for instruction

Figure 7.1. Focused Seating with Tables

you to face the students at all times (another preemptive method of behavioral management).

Figure 7.2 provides an example of the seating focus with desks. The lines here represent walking space and the potential for physical proximity, which is another consideration. Without the regimented rows, the ability to move about is much easier. However, the "deepest" row is about three desks.

The ability to monitor by physical presence is probably something you've read about. However, that physical presence must be within a reasonable proximity. Seats that may present a problem with using proximity are marked with an X, so if we were creating a seating chart, those seats would be filled in last.

For veteran teachers, take a look at your classroom layout from the perspective of discipline issues. Where, geographically speaking, do most of the issues seem to occur? How could you shift seating for more effective sightlines for

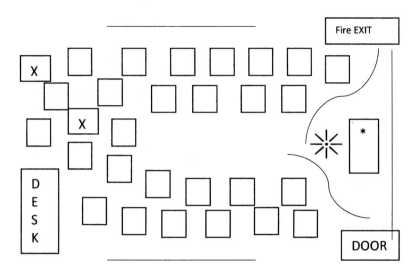

*   Overhead/student folder boxes
X   Potential problem areas/sightline issues
❇   General focus of class for instruction

Figure 7.2. Focused Seating with Desks

you and, thus, the students? Try to move away from the standard rows if at all possible. They have more impact on students than we may realize.

I behaved very differently in different classes solely based on the class's seating structure.

In classrooms that were arranged so that every student had a more up-front position, I found myself to be more active in the lessons, and I interacted more with the teacher and the other students.

Whereas in the typical block formation, where all students face the chalkboard, I felt more like a part of some vast machine without any discernible purpose for my singular perspective. I'd often become bored and easily distracted, floating between passionless lectures and test after test.

For the ideal classroom, students should feel that they are a part of a group where their interactions have merit. The environment, as created through seating arrangement, can have a strong impact towards that end. ~ Daniel

A final note on the use and placement of teachers' desks—your desk should not be a consideration for the learning space. It is your operating space for those times when students are *not* present. No seating arrangement should hinge on the location of your desk, and if cabling issues present themselves, there are always cable extensions. If the desk is keeping you from an optimal seating arrangement, do whatever you can to overcome that issue.

Prioritizing the *class* and not your *office space* will further emphasize your goals and vision for the class. The students will get the message that "My teacher puts *me* first."

We are all human, but the last thing a teacher needs to display is confusion about the classroom. If you're confused, then the students are confused. And where do you go from there? ~ Crystal

Seating Charts

After creating your physical seating arrangement and floor plan, you'll want to work on your seating charts. Seating charts are a necessity at any grade level (even seniors!), and any teacher who just allows students to take any seat on that first day is opening him or herself up to a year of anguish.

Last year on the first day of school, I let the kids pick their seats, and it was awful! I've read that you should let students pick because you don't know who they are and should trust them to make that decision . . . yeah, right! My first year I assigned seats, and it was so much better. Will always and forever assign seats on the first day! ~ Stacey

Using the floor plan of the classroom, choose the students' seats based on gender, race, parent/student information received, and known discipline problems. Separating boys and girls whenever possible is the first division for offsetting problems before they begin.

Separating racially, although some may consider it politically incorrect, has a definitive purpose when doing so for behavior. Moreover, it reinforces the idea that we are a "class" together, not a bunch of smaller, racial/ethnic groups. It also encourages a stronger class bonding as opposed to clique bonding. Most students won't even recognize the arrangement as an arrangement.

Figure 7.3 provides a potential seating arrangement, based on the divisions. It's admittedly cold and sterile. However, it's practical.

Should the students question your decision to use a seating chart (and some might), be prepared to explain it. You might say something like: "Mostly, it's for me. My goal is to learn your names in three days, and I'm someone who learns names by location. Creating your charts is how I begin to study them!"

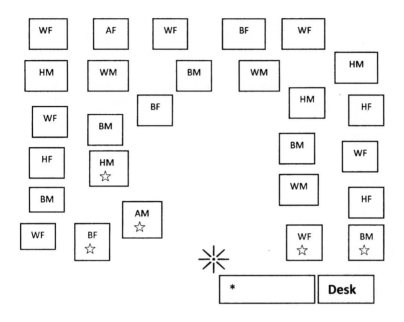

M/F: male and female
A: Asian
H: Hispanic
W: White
B: Black
☆ : Potential Discipline issues/known behavior problems

Figure 7.3. Floor Plan Gender/Race Distribution

This response accomplishes a couple of things: (1) it's difficult to argue against, and (2) it supports a positive response to a complaint. In subsequent years, once you've built up your confidence with this method, you might add: "We're going to be moving around quite a bit. Plus, this arrangement isn't set in stone. Let's see how it goes!"

Phone calls with parents will also help you out in determining placement. A visually impaired student, for example, will need front seating. A deaf student will need a good spot for both student and interpreter. Parents will also give you hints about their child's behavior, and those with attention and/or focus issues can be placed appropriately. You might even consider asking the student where he/she prefers to sit in your welcome call.

Additionally, students with known discipline problems or "reputations" should be strategically placed.

Shouldn't the students get to start off fresh for the new school year? Won't they perhaps misconstrue our intent? Are we judging them before we even meet them? ~ a high school teacher

Here's the thing—those students who are "regulars" in the dean's office know they have a reputation. However, since you've so disparately separated the class and created as many front-row seats as possible, they will have no idea that they are being strategically placed based on their behavior. At least, they shouldn't be able to perceive it.

The breakdown in Figure 7.3 results in:

HF: 3
HM: 4
WM: 3
WF: 7
BF: 3
BM: 5

Thus, the first distribution in this class would be White Females (the largest group), followed by Black Males. It's possible that your majority races or genders might be less varied. Separate as best you can. Start by leaving at least one or two empty seats between students.

When you're ready:

- Create a virtual chart in a document.
- Determine the *largest* group by gender and race for the particular class (15 BM, 12 WF, 4 AF, and so on).
- Distribute majority group, leaving at least one seat between them.
- Distribute second largest group, third, etc., until all seats are filled.
- Identify potential discipline problems and locate them nearest to your focal instructional point of the class.

It's important to remember, also, that this is only the *general* seating layout. Naysayers will note that girls are more or less further back. Yes, they are because in *general* (not always, certainly) girls are less of a behavior problem, and these first days of school when you are critically establishing the class, you need all the additional help you can get.

Numbering Seats

Your logic for numbering seats is up to you. However, *clearly* numbering the seats is a crucial step. This can be as fancy as a piece of paper with a number written on it and taped to the back of the seat (where the student's back rests and it can be seen easily at first glance). Masking tape and permanent marker will also work! Of course, the numbers may eventually come off, but they will have served their purpose by then.

Creating a list of numbers in a document and spacing them is a simple, quick way to create your seat markers. Have some fun with fonts! From there, cut with scissors or a paper-cutter. Double-check that you've numbered each seat.

The Student and the Seat

Of course, you can't stand at the door and look up every student and the corresponding seat for every class. Thus, creating a way that students can manage this by themselves is fun.

From your virtual floor plan, create an alphabetical list of students' names with their corresponding seat number for each class period. Handwrite the list, or type it and transfer onto an overhead sheet. (See Figure 7.4.)

Students find their names using the alphabetical listing. From there, they only need to determine your logic for numbering. They'll see the seats are numbered, locating them readily. This method has proven itself year after

Period Four

Name	Seat	Name	Seat
James A.	23	Preslin Q.	10
Jillian B.	12	Betty S.	30
Luke C.	5	Alex T.	19
Toby D.	2	Xavier V.	26
Costas K.	1		8
Lucy M.	10		20
Victor P.	28		16

Figure 7.4.   Seating Chart Identifier for First Days

year. Plus, it provides the student with a sense of accomplishment *before* you've even started to speak!

Leaving blank spaces next to open seat numbers will also provide you with the ability to easily write in new students or changes in students.

CREATING AN ATMOSPHERE

You can tell when you walk into a genuine teacher's room, can't you? There is a sense of uniqueness, love, and warmth exuding from the walls and shelves. It is a living paradox: homey and professional, peaceful and challenging. Consider that students tend to take better care of a room that they perceive to be "individualized." Thus, the atmosphere you create greatly contributes to your classroom management.

If you're unsure of what you want to do with your room, visit other classrooms to get some ideas. Ask friends who have that knack for decorating to help you. Obviously, posters are an excellent means of conveying your persona, but don't stop there. Frame your certificates and awards and proudly display them. Display former students' work (if you have it). If you're permitted, real or artificial plants help too.

TEACHER PRE-INSTRUCTION DAYS

Once we officially returned, our pre-service days were meeting after meeting. We had about an hour or two (if we were lucky) to be in our classroom. ~ Tori

Your ultimate goal will be to have the following items completed or near completion by the first day teachers are officially called back:

1. Welcome calls/preemptive communication with parents and students
2. Course syllabi and outlines
3. Physical class setup
4. Copies of all materials for the first week
5. Preliminary seating charts

As Tori reminds us, teacher pre-instruction days are inevitably filled with countless meetings, committees, and required in-service programs. Every school is different, but one thing's for sure: there is not a minute to spare! Bring your planner with you to all meetings so that you can include any relevant dates or information.

Having completed this planning, main communication effort, classroom organization, and copying, you will be able to concentrate on the inevitable, multitudinous new rules and/or changes for the school year.

For example, the school may foist a new syllabus on you. No worries! You'll be able to provide an addendum to what you've already done, which is far less time-consuming. Check for the "new" stuff, type it and slice it. Or, if it's a small enough change, consider having students write it in at the appropriate time. Either way, because you've already done the base work, you will be able to prioritize your time in picking up supplies, required forms, textbooks, equipment, and handbooks.

If you have any doubts about this approach so far, take a look at your colleagues after a day or so of pre-service days. They might fall into one of two camps: The "Mehhh, Don't Care" camp or the "OMG Stressed" camp. The former group is an apathetic bunch, and it's best to avoid them if at all possible. They dampen enthusiasm.

The OMG campers are exhausted, already starting their new school year feeling behind. Some of them will stay until eight or nine o'clock at night just to overcome that stress. They'll work the entire weekend before school starts. By waiting until the last minute to do all of their work, they are missing out on a personal sense of confidence and a crucial first impression time with their students.

RETRIEVAL OF EQUIPMENT

If you haven't already, introduce yourself to the media specialist and the computer techs. These are the individuals who can get you what you need for your classroom. They are also a valuable resource for information that may or may not be written down. All too often, schools have *unwritten* procedures that just don't make it into meetings or orientations, and these folks will be able to help.

Additionally, if you find that your school does not offer you the use of an overhead projector, consider finding a patron for your class. These projectors are less than two hundred dollars, and more than likely, you can find a willing business partner for this purchase if need be. It's a crucial piece of classroom management equipment.

OPEN HOUSE

If time allows, decorating the classroom for Open House is an enjoyable activity. However, a simple "Welcome" written on the board will also suffice, if that's all you can do. Since parents and students will have a lot of wait time to speak with you, consider what you can provide to keep them busy. One tactic is to bring candy or cookies—anything to convey your welcome.

Returning teachers might highlight projects from the previous year throughout the room, which lends a positive "showcase" feel to the environment. You might also play soft classical music in the background.

One year, my son joined me, bringing along his video games to play on the classroom television. Often, parents will bring younger siblings, so that kept the little ones somewhat happy.

Info Table

One table, prominently located, should be your main info table. Make sure to lie out business cards and welcome letters. Consider putting a sign-in sheet, with a spot for e-mail addresses, or contact sheets for parents to complete. There will be some duplication as you'll be handing these out on the first day, but it gives parents something to read and fosters questions.

It's up to you if want to provide your syllabus. If you've got plenty of copies, it can serve as fodder for conversation. However, since it will be available online, you may not have to.

The info table is also a good place to ask for donations of supplies. Create a "Wish List" on the table by placing several colorful sticky notes for easy pickup. On each sticky note, write what is desired:

—two boxes of tissues
—one ream of colored paper
—one ream of white copy paper
—masking tape
—cello tape
—dry-erase marker or colored chalk

If they are able, parents will take a sticky note as a reminder. By the end of the night, most, if not all, of your "wishes" will be taken.

Supply lists are up to you, as well. If you have more than three requirements, consider creating a list on colored paper. You can make four mini-lists on one page, make several copies, and cut them into quarters. Another option is to include the list on the syllabus.

First Impressions

Of course, you are going to be your charming best at Open House. You'll be dressed professionally, and your classroom will convey the warmth and enthusiasm you desire. You'll be smiling and happy as you put faces to names from your telephone calls. Hopefully, you'll have a high number of attendees since *you* have taken the time to call them individually. You will be an Open House success!

Talking to parents generally centers on the student or the class. However, you'll also want to do some reconnaissance for potential volunteer opportunities or guest speakers later in the year. For example, is one of your parents in a career that might interest students or that might connect nicely to a project you've got planned? (Another reason to do that planning ahead of time!)

The real trick to making conversation with parents is not talking at all, but asking questions. Let the parents or the students do the talking.

For freshmen:
Discuss schedules, locations, orientation, what student enjoyed in middle school. Is student new to district?

For sophomores and juniors:
Discuss what classes student liked last year and why, what both parent/ student would like to see the school improve upon, extracurricular activities. Is student new to district?

For seniors:
Discuss what classes student liked last year and why, what they'd like to see the school improve upon, what their plans are after graduation and whether you can be of any help. Is student new to district?

Altogether, these are not huge undertakings, but the message conveyed to students is:

This class is going to be fun!

and the message conveyed to parents is:

This teacher is professional.

Well, the prep stage is over. You've done all you can. You've got a vision, and you're a professional. You've preemptively begun to manage your class. You're ready to go with all copies and supplies. School starts tomorrow. Are you ready?

Chapter Eight

Judgment Day

The first day of class you greeted each one of us as we walked through the door into the classroom. In my experience, no other teacher had done that. It was such a simple, yet effective, idea that instantly told students you were directly engaged with them. ~ Crystal

Ah, the first day. Our honeymoon. The students are usually well behaved, and there is a feeling of excitement lingering in the air. Veteran teachers will tell you, "Mehhhh . . . just wait. It'll pass. Then you'll come back into reality."

What happens though, if we *refuse* to lose that excitement? What if we decide to capitalize on that excitement to lead in with an even stronger, more durable feeling in the classroom? The term "honeymoon" is completely apt because the relationship of the class to the teacher is analogous to a marriage. And just like a marriage, what happens *after* the wedding and honeymoon is what makes or breaks the relationship.

Although you may have spoken to students at Open House or in your welcome calls, this day *still* has a sense of beginning. Many teachers think they are building rapport on this first day, but what's actually happening is the students are listening and judging, the mere inklings of rapport. The authenticity of your persona and vision as well as your reactions to behavioral issues (should they present) are being evaluated.

Teachers tend to revel in the low or nonexistent behavior problems of this phase, misusing the opportunity by lecturing too long, talking too much, or jumping smack-dab into curriculum.

This first day can best be used by moving the attention off of the teacher as soon as possible. The ideal class is not about the *teacher*; it's about the *class*. Your choice of activities and purpose for this day will validate this vision.

Most students are going to make up their minds whether they're going to give you a hard time the rest of the year (or whether they're going to put forth any effort in the class) *on this day*. Luckily, though, you've gained an edge with some students with your welcome calls and possibly at Open House. To enhance this fledgling base of rapport, you'll want to consider how to convey your desires for the class along with your persona.

AT THE DOOR

Stand at the door. Greet each student with a handshake and a smile. I'll say that again: a handshake. That's what professionals do when they meet. That's how new bosses greet their new employees. Model the behavior you expect.

Do you know the student's name? Use it! Did you meet him/her at Open House? Reference it. Say: "Hello! You're . . . no, don't tell me . . . Victor, right? I remember you from Open House! (*shake hand*) Come on in, and please check the board and find your seat!"

Perhaps you haven't met the student yet. You might say:

> Hi! What's your name? Julio? Julio! I'm Mr./Ms._____, nice to meet you! (*handshake*) I don't think I got through to your home phone for a welcome call, so I want to make sure I have the right number! Will you make sure to write it down for me on the contact sheet? Thanks. Come on in, find your seat, and take a look at the board!

You've done this scads of times in the professional world. However, you may not have done this with students. Your goal is to welcome every student personally before he/she sets foot in your class.

Of course, you may have to deal with a new student/new seat on your chart. That's fine! If you "miss" welcoming a student at the door, then take the time to welcome him/her when you take attendance. Whatever you do, don't miss a welcome and a handshake.

> *Some teachers would be up at the front of the class as if at the pulpit in a church, not to be disturbed, only listened to. The class came in, sat down, and "bam!" we jumped into the syllabus, teacher expectations for the year, etc.*
>
> *That greeting is the student's initial encounter with the teacher (aside from Open House, if applicable)—plus, you can tell a lot by a handshake. ~ Christina*

Is this a lot of trouble to go to? Would it be easier to gather paperwork, look busy, and sound important? Perhaps. You can choose to build a foundation of rapport and strengthen your relationship with the class, or you can do your thing and hope for the best. The choice is yours!

FIRST DAY LAYOUT

The majority of students come in that first day lively, happy, and enthusiastic. After greeting them at the door, repeating their names, and referring them to their first task of finding a seat, you'll send your next message: "I'm *ready for you!*"

At each student's seat, have a manila folder, filled with relevant class forms and documents. Remember that conference where they had the nifty doo-dads and pens all set out at each place? It's wonderful to have stuff already waiting for you, isn't it? It makes us feel comfortable and secure. It also boosts our opinion of the presenters—these people come in early to make sure things are set up properly. They are exceptionally professional.

(As a plus, students like to draw on those folders. It gives them a "doodle-spot," potentially saving the desk/table tops from unwanted graffiti.)

As much as possible, allow students to self-direct. They may or may not catch on at first, but soon they will. They might see something like this written on one side of the board:

Today's Objectives

- Complete administrative requirements.
- Get to know each other!
- Practice Procedure Number 1.

And on another board or other side of the same board:

Welcome to Ms. Keller's Class! ☺

What to do:

1. Please find your seat number by looking at the overhead.
2. Please place your schedule on the table in front of you.
3. Please begin completing the yellow Contact Form.

The repetitive use of "Please" is intentional. Want politeness from students? Give politeness. Model politeness.

I liked how you had the notes on the board using "please." The teaching courses tell us to write things in the positive not the negative. However, you are telling us why, and that it works in a high school setting. ~ Stacey

Yes! I thoroughly enjoyed teachers who wrote the daily activities/what we're doing today on the board. That methodology captured me immediately. Aside from the fact that I cannot live without lists, I appreciated the fact that they took the time to tell me, the student, ahead of time what we were doing that particular day.

So many of my fellow students also appreciated that . . . it was always the first thing we looked at when we walked in the classroom. The writing on the board started the class off without anyone even saying a word. ~ Christina

Whether the students actually sit and complete the contact form or not is not something to dwell on at this stage. It is a *conditioning* point for helping students understand how to start class without saying a word. You're *conditioning* students to look at the board for information (which may seem like a no-brainer) because the mechanics of "doing" stick longer than the "telling." A student repeating an action every day, such as looking at the board first thing, is another means of management.

While it's important for a student to be able to reason for themselves, it's also important that they don't get stuck if they lose their way throughout the course of the lesson. Regular daily notations on the board manage to fulfill both. Students will be able to ascertain on their own what they need to be doing while also being able to use the board as a guideline to find their way back to the task at hand, should they drift away. ~ Daniel

The purpose for providing the students with something to do also begins the bonding process in the class. Somebody will see what's expected, and that someone will pass along the intel. Another, more subtle message is sent too: "I believe in your ability to reason."

In order to find his seat, the student must either *reason* for himself, or another student must reason that a classmate needs assistance. The lost student will look all around, and if he can't figure it out, inevitably, someone will help him, whispering, "Dude, you're in seat 27!"

Finding their seats is their first assignment, and they do (at this point, anyway) want to please the teacher. You haven't *told* them how. They've had to figure out amongst themselves. You have already begun to teach.

SELF-INTRODUCTION

The bell rings, and it's time to begin. The class may be boisterously loud or solemnly silent. Either way, you're up to bat first.

I remember the first day of drama with Ms. Keller. As a freshman I was about to jump out of my seat—the entire class was abuzz with chatter. And suddenly I remember thinking, "Shouldn't class have started by now? What's the deal?"

There was Ms. Keller, standing silently, watching us all with a little smile, and very calmly she said, "I'll wait." Eventually we elbowed each other into silence, but I remember sitting there mystified by this woman at the front of the classroom who didn't bang a desk or raise her voice to silence the classroom. It

may not have been as jarring as a teacher yelling but it was clearly effective—it
set the precedent for the remainder of my education with her. ~ Crystal

I had to decide what to say to Crystal's class at that point because they couldn't be held accountable for a procedure. They didn't know it. Again, modelling is the thing wherein you'll catch the conscience of a class. Do you want your students to yell? Then, you shouldn't yell either.

Introducing one's self is always a tricky thing. For the first few years, you may want to write it out and practice ahead of time in front of the mirror. Practice projecting the right amount of enthusiasm, cool headedness, and professionalism. In many ways, it's the response you might give a potential employer in an interview to the statement, "Tell me a little about yourself."

Take *no more than two or three minutes* to give them an overview of your education/experience, and interests—that's about all anyone can take of someone introducing him/herself, wouldn't you agree? Consider repeating your name at least twice, especially if it's long or difficult to pronounce. Emphasize how excited you are about what the class is going to do, in general, and then transition into calling attendance. Rehearsing this little speech will help with your nerves. Do it until you can exude a confidence that you didn't even know you had!

Your short introductory speech accomplishes quite a bit in the span of a few minutes. For veteran teachers, is it time to rehash your introduction? Is yours too long, too short? What do you actually say? Do you even know?

Another way to approach this first hurdle is to consider what you'd want your students to do if given an introductory speech for an assignment. Model your expectations. Set the bar high, and your students will follow.

I'm REALLY glad you are including what to say. My first two years I did not plan out what I wanted to say, and I was a blubbering idiot. I remember being so intimidated by my eighth graders this past year, I said, "I can be the cool teacher if you behave correctly."

Biggest mistake! I'm not supposed to be the cool teacher . . . ahhh, salt to the wound! New teachers need to realize that this needs to be written down and rehearsed so that they can figure out how they want to look and just feel prepared for the kids.

I also like the idea of keeping it short because most kids will not remember what you say on the first day, but those that are listening at least can get a feel for the teacher and the class. ~ Stacey

MY NAME . . . ME

Knowing a student's name is a powerful influence, and since mispronunciation is inevitable, don't gloss over it. State it: "I'm going to do my best pronouncing

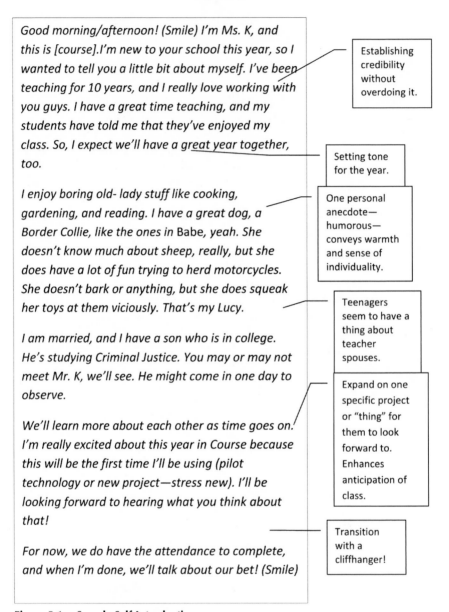

Good morning/afternoon! (Smile) I'm Ms. K, and this is [course]. I'm new to your school this year, so I wanted to tell you a little bit about myself. I've been teaching for 10 years, and I really love working with you guys. I have a great time teaching, and my students have told me that they've enjoyed my class. So, I expect we'll have a great year together, too.

Establishing credibility without overdoing it.

Setting tone for the year.

I enjoy boring old- lady stuff like cooking, gardening, and reading. I have a great dog, a Border Collie, like the ones in Babe, yeah. She doesn't know much about sheep, really, but she does have a lot of fun trying to herd motorcycles. She doesn't bark or anything, but she does squeak her toys at them viciously. That's my Lucy.

One personal anecdote—humorous—conveys warmth and sense of individuality.

I am married, and I have a son who is in college. He's studying Criminal Justice. You may or may not meet Mr. K, we'll see. He might come in one day to observe.

Teenagers seem to have a thing about teacher spouses.

We'll learn more about each other as time goes on. I'm really excited about this year in Course because this will be the first time I'll be using (pilot technology or new project—stress new). I'll be looking forward to hearing what you think about that!

Expand on one specific project or "thing" for them to look forward to. Enhances anticipation of class.

For now, we do have the attendance to complete, and when I'm done, we'll talk about our bet! (Smile)

Transition with a cliffhanger!

Figure 8.1. Sample Self-Introduction

your names, but I may mess them up. Please let me know (*indicate "one" with index finger*) if I've mispronounced your name, and (*indicate "two" with second finger*) let me know how you prefer to be called."

Taking the time to acknowledge that you may make a mistake is an important message. Also, taking a moment to ensure that the student is called by a preferred name conveys that you really want to get to know your students. Finally, the nonverbal indicators help keep your class engaged and listening, especially if you have students whose first language is not English.

For example, you might say, "Gerald Alsop? Gerald! You prefer Gerry— okay! G-E-R-R-Y, like that? Thanks. (*smile*)"

Smart aleck alert: If you have any smart alecks in your class, they will make themselves known at this time. Pay attention to who makes the comments. Look him/her directly in the eye, with a look that says, "I hear you. I like you, but I wish you weren't doing that. We're going to discuss this later." Don't verbalize anything at this point.

If possible, put a little dot next to that student's name so that you can reference the behavior later. As you call the student's name, get his/her information, give another meaningful, but *warm* look. Not an angry one, simply: "I'm aware. Don't worry, though. We'll be okay."

Once the first roll call is complete, tell the students about your goal of only calling attendance for the first three classes. Bet them that at the end of three classes, you will know at least 90 percent of their names. (This is another plus for seating charts as the student is in the same spot every class.) After those first three days, be prepared. You will not call attendance aloud.

> *By telling your students, "Hey, just so you know, I will know your name in three days," you've really told them, "I care about you."*
> *You're also making it a priority where other teachers do not do it that way. They may have it as a priority, but they don't announce it. They are missing out on an opportunity to show the students they really care about them and to set expectations in the class. ~ Tori*

PROCEDURE NUMBER ONE

Introduction, attendance, and any other administrative tasks are going to take about twenty minutes, if not more. However, you can then do something a bit more "fun" and allow for some movement.

Before you begin your icebreaker activity, which entails a lot of walking around and talking, introduce the students to "the Hand" or your way of quieting the class. If you're using the Hand, you might say:

Probably the one thing that drives teachers crazy is getting the class's attention. And probably, one thing that drives students crazy is teachers yelling at them to be quiet, right? I don't want to yell, and we have a lot of activities where we'll be discussing or moving around. So, this is how I like to get your attention (*demonstrate*). We're going to practice this procedure right after we mess around with our scavenger hunt.

While demonstrating, make eye contact with the class, *smile.*

Of course, you need the justification for practicing the procedure. It's helpful to do something goofy and fun on the first day. Why not? Your goals are to complete administrative tasks and get to know your students. You don't have many days to do that, so take advantage of the honeymoon phase with a fun icebreaker.

ICEBREAKER

Being in your class helped me see things a little differently. I started to try and get to know people more instead of making decisions about people based on what they looked like or what group they hung out with. (I also remember you being very tolerable with me; you gave me several chances.) It seemed to me that you wanted the best for your students from the first day. ~ Zach Russakis

The creation of a positive classroom climate is forged in these first few moments as the students begin to step out of their comfort zones in a safe way. It's imperative that the teacher understands the dynamics of the class, and to begin that understanding, you have to observe the students.

Much like a scientist, you'll observe them in their natural habitat during the ice breaker activity as they move about and communicate with one another. You'll see who your more reticent students are, who your potential "all-stars" are, and who your potential leaders are.

A search on the Internet will provide you with numerous possibilities for icebreakers. However, be extremely careful in your selections. You want the students to interact, but consider their dueling adolescent mindsets. They both desire and hate attention. They're scared and bold. Thus, the icebreaker you select should allow for the polarity and spectrum of their personalities.

Many teachers attempt an icebreaker by having students introduce themselves before everyone else. While encouraging interactivity in the class is good, it's unwise to put a student on the spot. Some of them don't care to be the focus of attention, and being made to do so can cause the student to harbor some resentment—ultimately counterproductive in the formation of an ideal class.

When a turtle hides in its shell, it tends to come out quicker if you let it do so on its own, as opposed to trying to force it. Activities that let the students choose their level of involvement will probably prove to be more effective as icebreakers. ~ Daniel

Icebreakers were always nerve-wracking for me in high school. Girls are still at that awkward stage of coming into their own and battling constant insecurities, so icebreakers are terrifying.

> *However, they're also the best possible thing for a fourteen-to-fifteen-year-old to participate in if the activity is group oriented. The first day, all students are in the same boat. What better way to "come together as a team" than an icebreaker? I wish more of my teachers would have incorporated this into the first day. ~ Christina*

One icebreaker that works very well in alleviating potential angst is the "scavenger hunt." It entails whole-class involvement and movement without anyone being singled out; thus, everyone's doing something, but no one is in the spotlight.

The goal is to fill in several blanks (usually twenty to twenty-five) on a document, with a person's name, such as:

1. Find someone who has more than fifteen pairs of sneakers. _____

Each student walks around the room and fills in the blank with another student's name. (Only using one name per blank—no repeats, and not their own name!) Include some more difficult ones that will require students to make a complete round of the class, for example:

2. Find someone who knows how to bake bread from scratch. _____

Additionally, since they are not allowed to use one student's name more than once, include one that is nearly impossible to find. Depending on your geographical location, a certain type of food (far removed from where you are) is fun:

3. Find someone who likes béchamel. _____

Only a certain type of person is going to know what *béchamel* is! (You may even have a student take the initiative to look it up in the dictionary that you will have prominently displayed.) Since students are not allowed to ask the teacher, they have to ask each other! By the end of the class, quite a few students will have learned something new *and probably made a friend!* ~ *Christina*

This icebreaker works especially well for large classes. It is very loud and very fun—the perfect setup for your use of the Hand.

While students are doing the scavenger hunt, you can take this opportunity to complete any administrative tasks such as signing schedules or gathering completed forms. This works much better than students "handing in" papers, which is time consuming and allows for too much downtime. Whenever possible, do routine stuff when students are *engaged*.

You can also use this time to follow up on smart-aleck commenters, if necessary. The whole class is involved in something, so talking to the student will go largely unnoticed by others. However, the point will be made.

When and how you discipline is critical for teenagers. Calling them out in public is ineffective. However, a quick, personal conference generally does the trick.

After about ten or fifteen minutes (or best judgment for completion of the task) use the Hand for the first time. Simply stand there, with your hand raised, a little above shoulder level (not way up in the air) and with a sense of purpose.

It will work, but give it a few minutes. It will also give you the opportunity to praise the class for following the procedure. *Smile. Praise. Compliment.*

Message received: "My teacher's way of quieting the class makes me feel good."

SPECIAL NOTE TO NAYSAYERS

Some teachers do have difficulty with this method. In most cases, it boils down to patience, or they simply forget to introduce it on Day One (Day Two is not as effective). Another possibility is that they don't use the appropriate nonverbal body language to accompany it.

Visualize a teacher standing there, with her hand raised, sighing in exasperation and rolling her eyes. This teacher might even be saying something like, "Okay, okay" or "Quiet."

Now visualize a teacher standing there with his hand raised, an expectant look on his face. His face says: *What should you be doing?* coupled with a semi-smile, not talking, content, patient.

Of the two, which one reflects a stronger expectation? Which one will compel the students to follow?

I will never forget the look in your eyes when that hand was raised. ~ *Christina*

You absolutely must stick to your guns with this gesture. Do not talk. Do not get angry. WAIT. Take the time to solidify this procedure with grace, poise, dignity, and professionalism.

Few lessons can be taught that are more important than "patience" (both for the teacher and for the student). The teacher who learns patience can easily teach it through exercise. As long as the teacher can endure, everyone, including the teacher, stands to gain from this lesson that is pertinent not only within the classroom, but within life as a whole. ~ *Daniel*

BRIDGING

The bridge of a song is that part of the music that's just a little bit different from the chorus or verses. However, it lends the entire song a sense of depth because it creates a sense of *building up* to something.

Your transition, or bridge, from point to point within the context of a lesson is there to provide a similar depth. Here, you're moving from a very fun, very loud activity to something a bit quieter. What do you say now that you've got their attention?

First, praise them and thank them. Be happy! Then, ask if anyone found the most "difficult" item, or someone who *really* bakes their own bread. In other words, chat them up about what they just did! Thank them again. Then, explain the next item.

Your bridge to the next objective for the lesson should be positive and warm, providing a pleasant, relaxing movement to the next point.

REMAINDER OF FIRST CLASS

The remainder of the first class should be dedicated to learning the students' names. Because everyone has been up and about, consider the "round the room" memory game, with yourself as the last person. (Person one says name. Person two says person one's name. Person three says one, two . . . and so on.)

By sparking the competition, with you as the last person who has to remember everyone's name, your students will love watching you squirm through the names!

Another powerful sense of community can be achieved through this. Unbeknownst to me, I had a mainstreamed ESE student with an IQ of about 70. We began working the names around the room, until we reached him. He struggled with the first few students' names. The silence made things worse.

And then, something beautiful happened. These teenagers, whom we are so quick to judge as apathetic and obnoxious, who could have made fun and teased, warmly and kindly offered their names to this young man. He repeated each one, one at a time. I'm not sure how they knew, but I'm glad they did.

Message received: "We are a class, *together.*"

END-OF-CLASS PROCEDURE

Five minutes before class ends, explain your end-of-class procedure and how you use it, whatever it is. You can then allow the class five minutes to prepare for the next class because you have your next class's layout to prepare for. The students will see you preparing for your next group. This unspoken observation is all part of your judgment day.

You'll also be able to talk to any students you haven't had an opportunity to talk to, asking questions such as, "Did you enjoy class today?" or "Where are you off to next?"

Message received: "My teacher is interested in me."

As the bell rings, thank the students for the class effort: "You guys did great work today! Thank you! This was a great class! See you tomorrow!"

Sometimes, the students will thank you too. Demonstrating gratitude to students further enhances the classroom climate and establishes your role as a transparent teacher.

Repeat as necessary for each scheduled class.
Transport self-unit home.
Put feet up.
Feel good.

You've made it through Judgment Day, and now, you're prepared for an intense first week!

Chapter Nine

The First Week

SETTING THE STAGE FOR STUDENT
EVALUATION AND INPUT

There's a special place in heaven for administrations that allow educators the *time* to cement procedures and discipline in that first week of school. The first week or so is where a warm, supportive classroom environment is born. Students get into the nitty-gritty of *how* an ideal class works before they begin curriculum.

When someone starts a new job, he or she doesn't jump into it. There is a time for preparation and observation before actually doing the work—a *training* period. This analogy definitely works for students and curriculum as well. By jumping into curriculum, we commit a tragic disservice to the creation of a class.

(*Note*: Granted, some schools have a preset agenda. Do the best you can with what you have. If nothing else, show your administrator this book. It may help!)

On Day One, the focus was introductions. Day Two shifts that focus to the class learning about each other. Please note, too, that the use of "Day" to separate these tasks is really for the sake of organization. If you have block periods, for example, you'll be able to combine the activities. However, the goal is to keep them *in this order* as best you can. They build upon each other.

DAY TWO

While Day One centers on the students judging you externally, Day Two makes or breaks the establishment of your class as an environment. You're going to breathe life into it by maintaining the persona you presented on Day One (or an even better, more relaxed persona) and by using the introduced procedures *consistently*.

Standing at the Door

Try to remember as many names as possible before the students enter the room and as you direct them to a defined task. This is a conditioning exercise.

Usually, you'll have an administrative task of some sort to have them complete. If not, find something quick and easy that is *not* curriculum related, such as an information sheet specifically for your class. The goal is to get them to walk in, grab their folders, and *do* something—in that order—in a positive manner.

What to say: As you stated on Day One, your goal was to learn their names as quickly as possible! "Hello . . . (*remembering/thinking*) Amy? Yes! Whoo-hoo! Grab your folder from the box and go ahead and start filling out your ___ (info sheet). Thanks!"

On the board:

Welcome back!

1. Please get your folder from the box.
2. Please fill out your ___.

On the overhead (if possible): the seating chart.

When the Bell Rings

Your first task is to use Procedure No. 1 to quiet the class. Walk directly from the door to the focus spot in the room. This use of the procedure may take a few minutes. Hold your ground.

Use your smile, stay calm. Above all, don't talk, *even if you're addressed*. If necessary, hold your finger up to your lips in a "shhhh" gesture, but don't actually make the *shush* sound. Wait. Wait. Wait.

Thank the class when they are quiet and praise them. They *will* get quiet. This gratitude and praise needs to tread a fine line between nonchalant and authentically grateful. You'll want to convey a sense of being exceptionally pleased with their performance and their recall of the procedure without hyperbole.

Telling high schoolers that they've done a "good job" with something this simple is akin to clawing your nails down the blackboard. It's demeaning. Try: *(smile)* "Thanks, guys!"

From there, you'll launch directly into attendance. However, you're going to make it a bit more interesting by reminding students that you've challenged yourself to learn all of their names by tomorrow (third class).

Today, you'll call their names, but tell them you *don't* want them to answer. You are going to *guess* where they are sitting. You may find this task a bit easier than your at-the-door exercise because of the seating chart!

The change-up for calling attendance in this manner is more interesting for them, and thus, they tend to sit quietly in anticipation. Not unlike hunters waiting to kill a wild animal, they'll want to see if you're going to "mess up." It's tense and fun! Because you probably *will* forget someone, make sure that you take that hit with dignity and poise—you're modeling how to react to a mistake.

Acknowledgment of New Procedure

After you've made it through attendance, acknowledge the class's new procedure. When you directed the students to get their folders and begin the task, they performed the Entering the Classroom procedure. More than likely, all of them did it, simply because you encouraged them to. Let them *know* they did a procedure:

> I want to thank you guys for doing the new procedure. The procedure for entering the class is to walk in, grab your folder, and look at the board (*demo as you say these points*). We'll keep working on this one, but I wanted to let you know that, hey, you did it already!

Administrative Tasks

If you have administrative tasks to complete, it's best to do these ditties first. Tell the students: "First there's something we need to do, and then we'll do something a little bit more interesting" (s*mile*).

Covering First Part of the Syllabus/Course Outline

Depending on the grade level you're teaching, you may want to consider "chunking" the discussions of your syllabus. Does it make sense to cover the entire syllabus for ninth graders? Maybe, maybe not. Frankly, you'll probably become a little bored towards the end and begin summarizing anyway.

While an eleventh-grade class may appreciate a heads-up about a large research project in the third nine weeks, students can't retain all of this stuff you've written, nor do they need to retain it. What they *can* retain, though, is the general outline of how things will work.

The presentation of the syllabus is definitely an issue that should be addressed. Teachers need to get students involved with the packet, not just read a list from a PowerPoint. That puts an entire room to sleep! How can you get students to be excited about what's to come? ~ Crystal

Another negative impact to covering the entire syllabus and class info in the first class is that you may convey a persona that isn't really you.

The first day of class I remember being handed a syllabus. It went over what was expected of us academically and her expectations. The first class she went over her rules. Everything was very clear and organized on how we were supposed to behave and what she expected from us, but I remember thinking that she was going to be a very strict teacher. I missed the old drama teacher terribly. She had a lot to live up to in my eyes.

The old drama teacher left us that year to take a job in a brand- new school. It was he who ignited my passion for the theatre. However, he was very relaxed in his teaching style and rules. So, when I was sitting in her class that first day, I was thinking, "Oh, there goes my favorite class." ~ Tori

The only positive message Tori received was the "clear and organized" point. Nonetheless, the mistake in her perception of my persona was made, and the class began on a negative foot, which was certainly nowhere near my intention! We had some issues that we resolved a bit later on, but probably, the issue began right here on that first day. Daniel's reaction wasn't much different:

Tori and I went through that same teacher shuffle, and I got a similar impression. That first impression, while very clean and organized, left me feeling concerned that the shift had taken a turn for the mundane monotony that made up the bulk of my classes.

Inevitably, and in short order, Ms. K would come to prove me wrong, but the impression from that first day initially caused me to question my choice of electives. In hindsight, however, her intent was both noble and clear, and I imagine the execution suffered greatly from her own nerves.

While the first impression may have been rough, it wasn't something that couldn't be overcome. Should another teacher come on too strong in introduction, remember that the progress towards the ideal class is not halted, merely hindered. Don't let a mistake or a setback keep you from achieving the ideal class you seek.

To persevere in spite of one's faults sends a more powerful message than one who proceeds without challenge. ~ Daniel

Thus, you see how noble intent doesn't necessarily do the trick. Not all students are willing to venture far enough in to even have hindsight. There's a huge difference between a teacher who *is* organized and one who *prides* him/herself on being organized. That's what these students saw: someone very ready to demonstrate how proficient and organized she was, but not necessarily someone who wanted to *collaborate* with them.

Determine, then, how you can present your syllabus in logical chunks. What information do they *need* to have and hear about? Here is the perfect opportunity to begin using your "Ask me a question" philosophy (which is addressed in more detail in chapter twelve). Students will have plenty to ask you about as it pertains to *how* you grade and what types of things the class will be working on.

You don't want to spend too long on the syllabus and course outline overview because it may cause anxiety. It shouldn't be the "big" part of your lesson today. Your ultimate goal is to convey a teacher who is willing to answer any and all questions, desires questions, thrives on questions, and who is truly enthusiastic about what he/she has planned for the course, all of which is your environment.

Break the Routine

At some point in the class, you'll need a stretcher sort of activity, one that will allow them to work freely and talk freely. This is a good opportunity for a quick ten-minute pair up/introduction activity:

The Best and Worst Teacher I Ever Had

You have their attention because you've just finished your syllabus and outline Q and A, so present what the class is going to do. Say:

> Okay! I've promised you something a little more interesting! *(smile)* In a minute, *(hold your finger up)* I'm going to ask you to find a partner *(put it down)*.
>
> You and your partner are going to describe the Best Teacher you ever had *(put one hand out to the side)* and the Worst Teacher you ever had *(other hand out to show balance)*. You'll want to take notes because you are going to introduce your classmate to the class and tell us about their experiences with their Best Teacher and their Worst Teacher *(hands again/smile)*. Now, ask me a question about this activity.

Wait. Make eye contact throughout the room. You should get a few questions, such as "Do we have to stand up when we talk?" The key is to wait. You'll know you've answered every question when someone finally says, "Can we start?" (Is that not music to your ears?) Then, you can say: "You have ten minutes—go for it!"

As the students are working in pairs, gather any relevant administrative paperwork. Also, use this opportunity to show them that you are not going to be a "stay up front" kind of teacher. You are going to stand behind them, among them, and perhaps sit down next to them in an empty desk/seat.

Yes! I remember you sitting down in empty seats. At first I was nervous about it, but as I grew accustomed to your teaching style I wished more teachers did it. It gave me (or my group) the opportunity to ask questions informally. ~ AnnMarie

I loved when you did this. Rarely did any of my other teachers take advantage of this ideology. When you sat down in our class, it made us feel as if we were all on the same level, even though there was this unspoken understanding that you were still the authority. ~ Christina

At the end of ten minutes, *gauge* their on-task behavior. Are they talking about teachers and experiences, or are they texting? The sound of an on-task class has a sense of urgency whereas an off-task class sounds "loose."

Check on those who claim to be done, and take a look at what they have. Talk to an individual student about what he/she's experienced. For example, if students tell you that teachers have taped their mouths shut, have them include some gory details, such as what it tasted like.

When the sound of the class begins to sound loose, use Procedure No. 1. Thank them for following the procedure.

You have their attention. Again, explain their choices for introducing each other. On a volunteer basis—don't call names—they have the option of both going up front, both standing at their seats, one sitting/one standing, or both sitting. (Now is not the time to quibble about formal presentation procedures.) The students will introduce each other and present the descriptions.

Generally, this is a bonding time for them because in some cases, they've come from the same feeder schools. Another component of the bonding is just the fact that they've all had good and bad teachers.

As the students talk about their experiences, make eye contact, show active listening, and take notes when appropriate. Sit down when students are introducing, whether that is on a stool up front or in a desk. Additionally, if the students go to the front of the class, consider removing yourself from the front.

Another idea, if you're comfortable with it, is having the students move their seats into a circle. Nothing breathes fresh air into a class more than a sense of "different" or "new."

Finally, initiate the applause ritual in the class. The students will be inclined to do so, anyway, but you will want to make sure the applause is vigorous for each pair by modeling. If you find the applause is somewhat weak, consider telling them: "Let's work on the golf-claps, you guys! We want to hear it for each group!" Have them do it again, smiling and nodding when they "get" it.

Make a conscientious effort to remember the really, really quiet students. Brand their faces in your mind, making notes about them. These are the kids whom we tend to forget and the ones we most need to remember.

End of Class

This activity will probably take you to the end of a one-hour class, so watch the time. A natural break will occur after a round of applause—people tend to be automatically attentive and receptive. When you have about three minutes remaining, stand up, remind them of the end-of-class procedure.

Thank them for a great class and great participation. *Remind them* to put chairs back in order, and let them have at it. As they are packing up and shuffling, take the opportunity to comment to students about what the class discussed—talk to them about their interests (whatever you can remember). Remind them of any end-of-class procedures.

When the bell rings, thank them again and *say good-bye. Smile, wave.* What you've accomplished today is multifaceted:

- You've established that you are dead serious about learning their names.
- You've also maintained consistency on your procedures.
- You've taught them another procedure or two without them realizing it.
- You've shown them that you understand the need for a stretcher-type activity.
- You've thanked them for their participation in the class.
- You've shown them you want them to get to know each other, an important component of any class.

DAY THREE

Standing at the Door

Again, try to remember as many names as possible *before* the students come into the room. Today is your last day to take attendance out loud! What's fun is that the students will come to the door with a smile on their faces because they know you are going to "guess" their names. They're already smiling! Such positive energy and you haven't even started.

What to say if you forget a name: "Okay, give me the first letter . . . just the first letter."

In between waves of students entering, watch for students who immediately go to the box to get their folders and thank them. "Thanks, Tom!"

For those students who don't seem to make it to the box, you might say, "Psst . . . Jenny!" and make a motion with your head for student to go to the box.

To those students who are walking past and are not in your current class (but in a different period), try to remember their names too. Smile and acknowledge them, but only talk to them if they talk first. (That seems to be the unwritten code.)

On the board:

Welcome back!

1. Please get your folder from the box.
2. Please fill out your ___. (Again, something administrative-ish.)

On the overhead (if possible): the seating chart.

When the Bell Rings

Use Procedure No. 1 to quiet the class. Walk directly from the door to the most obvious spot in the room, visually. This time, expect the procedure may take longer. Hard to believe, but true.

What students have learned is that teachers tend to start out with a "thing," but if students mutiny, the teacher tends to relent or give up. *You must not give up* on your procedures. These are the things that drive you crazy, remember?

Thus, no matter how long it takes, stand your ground with a smile on your face. Some kids may hold their hands up too. You may even get a high-five or two. (I was called the Statue of Liberty once.)

But no, you're Gandhi. You're Mother Teresa. You're the guy from *Kung Fu.* Do not become frustrated. Do not make any face other than one that conveys, "I'll wait for you because I know you can do this. I expect you to do this."

If it helps, consider that you are not yet teaching curriculum. The pressure to finish a lesson does not yet apply. You have the time to wait for them to fall in line. (*Note:* The longest I ever had to wait was three minutes, and it never happened again.)

Thank the class when they are quiet, *no matter how long it takes.* Refrain from being sarcastic, condescending, or patronizing. They must feel the authenticity of your gratitude coupled with a professional demeanor oozing out of your pores. You are calm and cool—unflappable in your procedures.

Your mantra: *I . . . am a calm, cool cucumber.* (Well, it might bring a smile to your face, if nothing else!)

Does this take effort? Absolutely! It takes more effort *not* to react than it does to react. However, this effort will pay off for an entire school year by saving you valuable time and stress. This effort is nowhere near as difficult as the effort to recoup.

Last Day for Attendance

Remind the class that this is the last day that they will see you take attendance. Henceforth, you will do so at a separate time and not at the beginning of class. Make a big deal out of this! *Whisper* their names, instead of calling them out loud.

- Look at the first name.
- Scan the room until you see him/her.
- Point to him/her, smile, and whisper the name.

What you're doing, somewhat unconsciously, is keeping the class quiet. They may talk a bit, but more than likely, since you're whispering, they'll whisper too.

Discussing the Remaining Procedures, the Rule, and Equity versus Fairness

You still have a few procedures to explain to the students. It may be that you even have the opportunity for a "live" introduction to a new procedure. For example, if someone asks to use the restroom or if someone is late, all the better! Use the moment. Ask the student (quietly), "Do you mind if I teach the procedure about using the restroom with you?"

Complete any leftover procedures and after you're finished explaining procedures, use the "Ask me a question" strategy.

When transitioning into the rule discussion, help students understand that the rule differs from the procedures in that there are consequences for breaking the rule. However, you haven't listed any consequences for the rule. Here's where it gets interesting when working with teenagers: the dance of youthful, intelligent *veracity* versus confident *sagacity*.

The students will immediately get the whole idea about the procedures, and they like knowing ahead of time that you're not going to yell at them for forgetting a procedure. They don't *believe* you, but they understand that, ostensibly, they won't get into "trouble" for forgetting to do something.

When introducing the rule, you're going to sense their skepticism, their sense of "Here it comes—hah!" Thus, introduce it as cryptically and nonchalantly as you can:

Now, I do have one rule, which you see here. I also have it behind me, here, on the wall. I think you'll find it very fair. The rule is a little different from the procedures, though. If you choose to break the one and only rule we have, then we have to deal with that.

Then, start shuffling papers or something, just to let the tension build until someone, inevitably, asks: "So . . . what happens if we break the rule?"
(Bingo!)
You might say:

Well, I guess that depends on what you do. I really don't know what my response will be until the rule has been broken. My goal, though, is to make sure that whatever you do and whatever I do *match*.

It's a weird way to think about it, I guess, but I won't treat you all equally. However, I will treat you fairly, when it comes to the rule.

Now, you will have piqued their interest. You might get a question at this point that will lead nicely to a hypothetical scenario. (That's where you want to go!)

Scenarios work best if you start off silly. For example, ask for a volunteer to help you out with a scenario. Ball up a piece of paper, hand it to the volunteer, presenting the following setting: "All of you are doing group work, and you're almost finished. (Student) is feeling a little silly and throws a paper ball at me."

The volunteer should oblige (be prepared for giggles and encourage applause). Then ask: "So, what is a fair response to this action?"

This will give them pause because it is on the disrespectful side of things. You might get a few responses along the lines of "Ask him/her to apologize, pick up the paper ball."

Acknowledge and validate their ideas. This is when you will hear their reasoning come out. Yes, you'll get some silly answers. Be careful how you treat those silly answers because these are, potentially, the students who can easily move into disruptive behavior.

Even when you hear the answer that works, ask for another volunteer. In other words, don't stop the discussion when someone "gets" the teacher answer—the goal is multifold: introduction to your rule, your methodology, and your manner of receiving responses/student input. Playing "Teacher Answer Wins" is not going to be in your repertoire.

Present a different scenario for throwing the paper ball (without an actual demo, but using the volunteer's name): "In this scenario, (student) is doing so because he's actually throwing the ball at (student). The ball hits me, instead. What do I do?" Take responses. Then, turn the tables on the students:

Does it make a difference if it occurs while I'm giving *instructions*? Why? What is a logical response to someone throwing a paper wad at someone else and who just really has bad aim? Does it merit a referral? A detention? A "talk" outside? What if he's done it ten times?

You may feel uncomfortable using yourself as the "stool pigeon" in these scenarios. However, in that vulnerability, you're showing a confidence in the class. If you can't do it, ask yourself why. Why can't you allow for this learning experience? What do you fear?

That vulnerability boils down to respect. You're demonstrating that you respect them and what they bring to the table. ~ AnnMarie

When these scenarios are enacted as learning experiences, the result is a warm learning environment. It is made warm by your confidence in yourself and your students.

Finally, you'll move towards discussing some events that did merit serious consequences. Students love to hear stories about other students and classes! Of course, you won't use names, but telling them about what you had to do when a student became aggressive towards another student will help them understand where the line is drawn.

"Story time" was always one of my favorites, regardless of grade! When the teacher told a story about a previous class or such, it was personal. It kept me focused and helped build a relationship between my teachers and me beyond the capabilities of any robotic lecture.

While listening and asking questions, not only would I get the point behind what the teacher was trying to accomplish, but he or she would also begin to gain more of my trust. ~ Daniel

When you indicate the consequences, you'll want to convey sadness and disappointment. Your students need to feel that you really don't want them to leave your class or be punished. The end message is: "My teacher gives logical consequences if the rule is broken."

End of the Class

Remind students that tomorrow you can't let them into class until you remember their names. Request that they not tell you. Remind them of the end-of-class procedure. *Thank them* for a great class and great participation. Remind them to put chairs/desks back in order, and let them have at it.

As they are packing up and shuffling, take the opportunity to comment to students about what was discussed. When the bell rings, thank them again and say good-bye. *Smile and wave like the folks at home.*

DAY FOUR

This is your D-Day! Do you know all of your students' names? Did you study them? Did you try to visualize them just by their names and the seating chart?

This is your first "test," and it roughly parallels what we expect of students. Thus, you must do your best!

At the Door

Try to have fun with this. Students whose names you remember can go in. Those who you don't remember, ask them to stand to the side but not to go in just yet. After all the recognized students go in, take a look at the remaining students. More than likely, these will be your quiet students.

If you're very brave (and a good actor), pretend not to remember one "loud" student, who's used to being remembered. Ask each student to give you a one-word clue. You'll probably remember 50 percent. Ask the remaining students to give you another, longer clue. More than likely, you'll have them all.

When you let in the last student, bring yourself into class with a sense of immense satisfaction. You may not even have to use the procedure on this day if you make enough of a commotion over your victory. You might consider:

"Thank you, thank you!" *taking a grand bow*
"Yes!" *walking in with a little strut*
"Tah-Dahhhhh!" *walking in with arms spread wide as though expecting applause*

The important thing is to show that you're pleased with yourself, and well you should be! Many students have complained that their teachers in high school never knew their names.

> *One of my teachers didn't know our names, and as a student, I knew that's why it led to so many classroom disruptions. There was no sense of community, and we didn't trust her to teach us. ~ Stacey*

Heads-Up for Quiz Tomorrow

More than likely, you have their attention from the applause or acknowledgment of your victory. If not, use Procedure No. 1. Because you've gone over all of your general procedures and the rule, it's time for the final quiz. Tell students they need to memorize the seven (however many) procedures and the rule for the quiz. If they ask what kind of quiz or the format, say, "All I will say is, most, if not all, of my students enjoy taking this quiz." Otherwise, let them think it's a usual humdrum sort of quiz.

Teacher Expectations

An enjoyable part of this first week is having the individual classes provide their expectations of the teacher. This event was prefaced with, "Now that I've told you all of my expectations for *you*, it's your turn!"

You should stress that you are aware that you are not perfect, and you always want to make sure you're meeting their expectations. This level of transparency is usually undiscovered territory for adolescents. When has an adult ever asked them about their expectations?

You were the first teacher who asked, "What do you expect from me?" That was, is, and will always be one of the most pivotal questions of my life. For the first time in my young adult life, someone wanted to know what I expected of them.

Students go through so much of their academic career being told what is expected. Giving them a positive environment based on mutual respect can be life-changing. ~ Crystal

Students react in a variety of ways to this sort of transparency; some are skeptical, some are absolutely silly, and others embrace it. The mindset of the adolescent works in your favor here: all teenagers love to give their opinions of teachers. Either way, the end result allows you to begin gauging the emotional needs of the class and the potential climate you want to create.

First, have students write individually on the topic—a "quickwrite" works well, which by virtue of the name alone seems to alleviate their stress of writing perfectly. Their prompt can be:

- What do you expect from me, as your teacher, and this class?
- What are some things you think a good [English, Algebra, History, etc.] teacher should never do, and why?

Purposely, don't give them a minimum or maximum to write because you can use this opportunity to determine who your *thinkers* are. If you're an English teacher, you might also note that on this particular assignment, you will not be grading for grammar or punctuation. This approach relaxes them and garners more authentic responses, which is your goal.

After students write their quickwrites, the papers can either be collected (if it falls at the end of class) or held onto for the next step: collective thinking. This will be the students' first group assignment, and as a first group activity, it puts everyone on equal footing.

For the group work, explain that you want them to work with their immediate neighbors. Your justification is that throughout the year, they will have different grouping methods; this will be "the easiest for everyone today." Before you start, though, discuss the expectations for what they will do.

One strategy that seems to help keep the flow of the class moving is to *write* the expectations in annotated format while you say them or *uncover* them on the overhead. The sense of uncertainty as to what comes next takes away the doldrums of hearing stuff simply read aloud. You might say, "In a minute (*one finger held up*), I'm going to ask you to create groups of four or five."

(*Note:* You might be wondering why the specific hand gestures are included. Be aware that the simpler the motion, the more attentive the response. This "in a minute" motion keeps them at bay until you want them to ask questions.)

On the overhead, write (or uncover): Groups—four or five

Make your way through all of the expectations, which are written out here in long form:

- The group should to be composed of four or five students.
- The group should reach consensus on the expectations of me as their teacher. (Note that the definition of *consensus* may be required.)
- The group should reach consensus on things I should never do, and be prepared to explain why I should never do them.
- The group is to provide at least three potential "consequences" if I do something I should never do.
- The group is to write a recap of their thoughts on a piece of paper or on a transparency.
- The time limit for this activity is twenty minutes.
- Each group will present their findings.
- Enthusiastic applause for every presentation.

Before moving on to the next item on the list, you should use "Ask me a question." At the very end, request questions again, until they are chomping at the bit to do something.

So, they'll huddle up in groups of four or five. Encourage the moving of desks/tables to ensure a stronger sense of the group. It's noisy, but the mood will be one of excitement and hope, which stems from this message: "My teacher really wants to do a good job for this class and me."

Wander about between the groups, handing out papers/markers, and answering questions. Enjoy sneaking a peek at what they've written so far. Inevitably, some will want to surprise you, covering their papers and whispering with each other, which lends further energy to this assignment.

Give them a five-minute warning by making eye contact with one group member and flashing five fingers, *silently mouthing* "Five minutes." Four fingers/four minutes, and so on, until it's time for the Hand to go up. Your impulse will be to try and speak over the din, but do your best to resist. Whenever you *can* use something silent or nonverbal, take that option.

On a volunteer basis, have groups stand and present. Another diagnostic aspect of this assignment is determining who the more confident students are because, generally, they are the ones designated to speak, or the ones who will talk the most.

This is also an exercise in patience on your part because it may take a few minutes to get volunteers. Have a legal pad with you, and look like you're writing something official while you wait. If you've offered them the option to remain at their seats, your volunteers will be more forthcoming.

Make notes while they present. After each presentation, the whole class should applaud. Again, if they don't clap loudly enough or enthusiastically enough, do it again. Even if all they did was stand up at their seats, they got the recognition for doing what they were comfortable doing on that day.

DAY FIVE

Armed with expectations, rules, and consequences, you'll all move to class consensus. On the overhead, jot down shortened versions that everybody agrees on.

General Expectations

Most, if not all, of the expectations will be on teacher "niceness" or level of "fun-ness." You'll also have some more specific expectations from students, such as "help us get better at writing" or "show us how we can do better on tests."

Sometimes, their expectations will be a bit less concrete. For example, they might say, "Teach us how to do good in geometry." If their expectations are too low or too vague, have the class clarify, but don't spend more than a minute doing so. If you delve too long or too deeply here, the class will get bored and boring.

I remember doing this expectation assignment! I loved how you asked what we wanted from you. I remember giggling and really enjoying what other groups said as well. This is a really great activity, and I'm definitely going to do it this year. ~ Stacey

Eventually, you'll have something like this:

We expect our teacher to:

Be on time for class.
Return assignments to us within __hours/days.
Be happy to teach us.
Be knowledgeable about what she/he's teaching.
Answer our questions completely or explain why she can't.
Do different things in class, not always the same thing.
Be fair.

Sometimes, you may find that students aren't demanding *enough*. For example, you might ask them, "You know, we expect *you* to be on time. What about me?" or "We expect homework back within a specified amount of time. Why shouldn't you have that expectation of me, depending on the assignment?"

The most difficult expectations were the behavioral ones. This reiteration of having expectations for the teacher does not, as some might presume, give the students authority or power. Rather, it sends the message: "My teacher cares."

Teacher Rules

Here is where the classes will probably unanimously and inevitably agree. Oh, they'll love these rules! You might end up with:

Rules for the Teacher:

No yelling.
No swearing.
Be polite and respectful.
No homework on Fridays.
Let us redo tests and assignments to get a better grade.

Most of the time, their rules will be fair. Of course, they'll try to get in the "No Homework At All" rule, which never does fly. You might agree, though, to a Friday thing. Why not? Longer assignments and projects will be assigned weeks in advance, and shorter assignments can easily be rerouted to during the week.

You can always wedge in a little disclaimer: *Unless absolutely, positively, and with class consensus, we agree to have no homework on Friday.*

Students, parents, and our entire culture have embraced a horribly nega-tive stereotype of teachers, and this sharing of expectations is another step of transparency. Your acknowledgment and analysis of how teachers *are perceived* versus how *you desire to be perceived* will make a difference.

You want them to understand that you take your job seriously, not with anger towards students, but with a righteous anger towards those who have made the teaching profession a joke. Emphasize that the worst teachers are not the ones out there beating students with erasers. The worst teachers are the complacent, apathetic repeaters. These are the ones who really bring down the profession.

Also emphasize that you are not here to judge other educators; rather, you are merely setting the bar of your expectations where you want them to be. You are simply *you*.

The goal is to begin developing a relationship that fosters a sense of trust, and in this activity, that seed of trust, which you've worked so hard to plant earlier on, is now beginning to grow.

Teacher Consequences

The consequences, which might range from a pie in the face to dropping the lowest grade for every student, usually take the longest to agree upon. This is such a fun way to end a class though! Some examples might be:

- A pie in the face during lunch (author's favorite)
- A bucket of water dumped over the head after school
- Free day (student favorite!)
- An "A" for everyone on an assignment
- Go down on knees and beg forgiveness from the class

The more creative these are, the better. (*Note:* this author did take a pie in the face one year.) Take your consequences willingly and humbly because, by gosh, if you break the rule, you'd better be prepared to walk your talk!

At the end of their discussions, remind them about their quiz, thank them for their participation, praise them for working well in groups and whole-class discussion, and thank them for a nice class. Of course, they will still need reminding of the end-of-class procedure.

DAY SIX

Your role after the class reaches consensus on expectations for the class is to create a sort of class creed, which you will read aloud and all students will review and sign. It can be placed in their class box for posterity. This ritual cements the deal: we are of one accord—we are now a *class*. As promised, you then move into the quiz.

Procedures and Rule Quiz

One of the most enjoyable moments of using the procedures and rules quiz is the display of student mastery. Since you haven't told students the nature of the quiz, all they know is that they are going to have one. Give them five minutes to cram.

Then, they should put all of their stuff away and listen to how the quiz will proceed. Each student selects three strips of paper, out of several, from a "hat" (think figuratively, if necessary). The strips can be typewritten (simpler to make and cut out) or handwritten as indicated in Figure 9.1. Read a couple of examples, including the "Break the Rule" demo strip.

Of course, Break the Rule is very interesting and entertaining, but the possibility exists for an "over the line" demo. Emphasize to students that they must demonstrate within reason. Most of them will do really silly, light-hearted stuff or mimic something appropriately.

However, in the case that a student does do something over the line, consider this scenario:

This student grabbed another student's backpack and threw it across the floor. We discussed that he had actually crossed the line in his demonstration, and he apologized, without prompting, to the other student. We also discussed the possibility of something broken, and the student checked her bag. Thankfully, all was well.

We then had a discussion on what might have occurred if something had been broken. Was "I" responsible, or the student? Why? Eventually, we came to the conclusion that as teacher, I would have been responsible, and rightly so.

This particular incident changed how I set out the logistics of the quiz. They had some parameters when it came to breaking the rule, and I used this incident as a non-example. ~ Mindy

> Demonstrate the procedure I use to get the class's attention.

> Demonstrate the procedure for when you are *tardy*.

> *Break the rule.*

Figure 9.1.   Sample Rule/Procedures Quiz Strips

You'll know you're making progress in the breaking down of barriers when students would feel comfortable enough to use you in their demonstrations. I was flicked, poked, yelled at, you name it. However, these actions were a demonstration of trust. Even so, if they occur, you'll hear the class hold its breath. All you'll say is, "Thank you."

Request silence from the moment a student takes his/her strips until he/she finishes all three. Talking *in between* demos is okay, and that knowledge seems to help them control their impulses. Tell them your rationale, "Hey, isn't it more fun to do it this way? You don't want a handwritten test, and neither do I! Ugh!"

Request applause after each demonstration. Some folks question the viability of this approach, but consider the positive outcomes: (1) the students were confident in their grades for this quiz; (2) they had fun; (3) the significance of the procedures was emphasized; and (4) students started out the year with a "high" grade. The message received: "This class (and teacher) can be somewhat interesting."

CONCLUSION OF FIRST DAYS

You've done a lot in this first week! Keep in mind that it is important to build upon the class *in this order and sequence*. Each activity is a bit deeper, a bit stronger, a bit closer—a purposeful progression. In other words, you can't leap into a procedures quiz without having learned names. You can't lurch into teacher expectations on the first day—it's too much.

> *Very important stuff here!! There must be a routine in place so that, as a student, you know what is expected and when it is expected. If you know to pass your paper to the person to your left, then the person at the end passes them up, then the teacher collects them from the front left person, well that certainly makes it easier. I found that this manner seemed to work well for many of my classes.*
>
> *A method that several teachers used that was not effective was an in-tray, labeled by class period, as you walked in the classroom to put homework in. This created a hassle and a funnel effect because students only have so much time to change classes. All of this needs to be worked through along with the students. ~ AnnMarie*

If your administration does not give you the necessary time to complete all of these tasks, then work through as many as you can, with the learning of names and completing the procedures quiz as priority. The complete list of activities is as follows:

Names
Best/Worst Teacher Intros
Teacher Expectations
Teacher Rules
Teacher Consequences
Class Creed
Procedures Quiz

You have skillfully prepared your students for your presentation of curriculum, and by doing so, your movement into coursework is going to be so much more pleasurable. Of course, you'll have to do a lot of reminding about procedures. Hopefully, you've had some fun and begun to understand the intricate personality of each individual class. Your transition to curriculum will be a rich experience!

Chapter Ten

Learning Versus Teaching

A TRANSITION LESSON

One of the reasons that students misbehave in class is that they have absolutely no interest in learning whatever is being covered. Kids will self-regulate only if they've invested in the lesson.

There is almost nothing a teacher can tell a class that will make them want to learn unless that teacher shows them that the information does—and will—have an impact on their immediate life. ~ veteran teacher

Telling the student that the material is important is not enough, though. Aiding them in discovering how the subject is important is what will increase their drive to learn. ~ Daniel

Thus far, you've worked hard to establish a rapport with your students. You've learned their names, and you've used them consistently and often. You've established a sense of unexpectedness and shown that you desire things to be as interesting and worthwhile as the students do. You've worked together to create a class, and you will soon be moving into the actual work.

The choice of a transition assignment is a crucial one. Keeping the discussion explicitly focused on the process of the class not only encourages interest, but it also *discourages* misbehavior. Teenagers enjoy discussing, analyzing, and evaluating their class experience, and in order to maintain transparency, this transition assignment helps to create a more effective bridge to curriculum.

Asking students for their interest in the process of the class encourages them not only to think but to want to learn. If they feel that the teacher is interested in what they think of the process of the class, they'll be more inclined to want to be a part of that process. ~ Christina

Before students can even begin to dive into the curriculum of your course, they must first understand the difference between *teaching* and *learning*.

We informally surveyed some seniors with this question: *What is the difference between teaching and learning, in your opinion?* Here's what they had to say, verbatim and *sic*:

Learning is the process of being taught.

Let's just say that teaching doesn't require staying up late at night and even in the morning to do homework.

If you're teaching you should be showing someone how to do something. If you're learning then you are being taught on how to do something.

Teaching is when they try to explain something to a student, and learning is when you find out something new.

Teaching is someone showing you how to do something, and learning is understanding what someone is showing/telling you.

Teaching is sharing the knowledge; learning is gaining and retaining the info.

If you're teaching, you already know what you're saying. If you are learning then you're trying to acquire the same knowledge as the teacher.

Teaching is describing and learning is absorbing.

Kinda, I'm lazy, more willing to teach.

These are the thoughts of a group who has watched teachers doing their thing and students doing their thing for almost twelve years. And their responses mirror those of every class with which I've worked.

Generally, student definitions of teaching are very ambiguous, misguided, or negative, but they seem to have a better idea of what teachers do than what they do as learners. Why? And, more importantly, how does their understanding of the concept impact their learning?

They don't know what they're doing, not because learning isn't happening or hasn't been happening for twelve years, but because they have never been asked. Thus, it's far more difficult for students to describe the concept of *learning*. Even more difficult is the concept that they are responsible for learning.

Obviously, teachers are responsible for teaching, but students are ultimately responsible for what *they do* with what *we do*! (Water. Horse. Drink.) You get the idea, but your goal is to get them to buy into it by coming to the conclusion themselves. It does no good to state it outright.

By engaging students in a dialogue about the two most important concepts of the class experience, you'll help them better understand their role within it. You've already presented your expectations of them, agreed on their expectations of you, and now they'll need to figure out their expectations of themselves. And here's how you'll do it.

THE FIRST DISCUSSION

You can use a variety of methods to begin this discussion, depending on where the activity lands during class (beginning, middle, or end). Take them along with you on the journey by noting, "Last time we [did a quickwrite] so this time, let's ____. Then, you can let me know which way works best for this assignment!"

For example, it could be a Venn-diagram *homework* assignment, leading to a whole-class discussion for the next day (end). Or, you can simply start from scratch with a whole-class discussion (beginning).

An interesting strategy for a middle-of-class discussion-starter is a Class Symphony. You pose a question (in this case, the teaching/learning question). However, you ask the class to respond all at the same time. That is, *they all speak as if they were the only one speaking.*

What happens is they voice their thoughts without fear because no one is able to listen to them. It's noisy, and if combined with a stand-up-and-stretch moment, you've effectively moved to a new topic within a lesson. Give them a minute or so to vocalize their thoughts.

Wherever it falls, strive to balance this discussion hook with how you approached the teacher expectations. For example, if you've used a quickwrite already, don't do that here. Think of something different.

It is in this experience, most likely, that the need for discipline will emerge because it is when the students must really start to think in terms of what they are responsible for. They sense the shift that's coming. Soon, they'll be working, taking tests, doing homework. They've been having "fun" up until now, so they may rebel against this movement to curriculum.

Thus, you'll want to make sure you express that on this first in-class grade; you'll be grading them on *how well* they handle themselves in discussion.

If the teacher has:

- previously handled student input/feedback on the class as an entity
- consistently and authentically presented a credible persona
- practiced and exercised examples of discipline and functional expectations
- heeded or, preferably, *exceeded* the students' expectations of him/her, to this point
- clearly modeled and explained the assignment
- presented the assignment's significance to the theme/unit/course
- extracted as many questions as possible

then, the students are more apt to be ready to move into their responsibility of learning.

THE *OUTSIDE* LESSON:
TEACHING WHOLE-CLASS DISCUSSION

Even though you've already had whole-class discussions of a sort, this is the first time you'll be formally addressing the discussion procedures. To create your discussion procedures, you'll want to think about what *you* want from a discussion. What do you see students doing? What are you doing? What does the "World's Best Class Discussion" look like? Whatever *that* is, create procedures that will bring it.

One of my pet peeves (and I'm sure one of yours) is that not all students participate in discussions. But how to "regulate" it? Another issue is that students really don't know how to disagree with one another tactfully. They'll interrupt or exhibit poor manners.

Enter your triple-layer lesson: a lesson on whole-class discussion, comparative analysis, and teaching versus learning.

First, provide the students with Discussion Protocol via the overhead, blackboard, or handout. Figure 10.1 would give students a tangible reminder of how to agree and/or disagree.

One thing you'll notice is the asterisk-challenge identifiers. Capitalizing on an adolescent's competitive nature is a tricky thing, but in this instance, each student is going to compete with him/herself. It's the first of many *self-challenges* that you may present, and how you present it is key. For it to be effective, it must be an internal decision.

How many students do you think might go for the challenge noted, without you having to really do much of anything? After all, you don't know what is or is not challenging to the individual student—only he or she does. Allow them the opportunity to challenge themselves.

Then, informally discuss *how* to discuss. Stress that some of these points are reminders, but others might be new to them, such as "yielding the floor." And here's another crazy idea: do not ask students to raise their hands. *Gasp!*

Remember our adult class that we're using as a model? Sometimes adults raise their hands; sometimes, they don't. Either way works for them. Thus, the skill of yielding the floor (which some adults are still working on, mind you), must be explicitly taught.

Modeling will be required in this instance, so consider asking for two volunteers. One volunteer will ask a simple "why" question on any topic. It's best if *you* provide the question. For example, "Why is the sky blue?" You and the other student volunteer will answer at the same time.

However, *you* will show how to yield the floor, and the other student can then give his/her answer. That student can then "give" the floor back to you

Discussion Protocol

Discussions work best when everyone participates!

Disagreeing with someone does not mean you need to be *disagreeable*.

Remembering the rule in discussion demonstrates maturity.

Some helpful phrases to use when discussing:

When you agree:

> *I agree with _____ because. . .*

> *Just like _____ said, it is. . .***

When you disagree:

> *I see your point about ____, but I have to disagree on. . .****

**somewhat challenging

***challenging

Figure 10.1.   Discussion Protocol for Handout or Overhead

with a gesture or a nod. Students have seen this, of course, but more than likely, they've never taken notice or analyzed it. That's where we're headed.

Students may or may not have the tools to agree and disagree effectively, so present them with some. They'll have the protocol right in front of them throughout the discussion (either on a handout or on the overhead), and your role, in addition to facilitating the discussion, is to teach how to discuss, explicitly encouraging when they forget and explicitly praising when they remember:

"Oops! Wait guys. George, would you say that again and use 'I have to disagree because . . .' please? Thanks."

"An excellent strategy for disagreeing, Juanita!"

"Beautiful supportive agreement, Keisha!"

"One of you needs to yield the floor, please. How do you want to handle that?"

Again, you'll only find success in this sort of assignment if you have lain the groundwork of persona and rapport. Your lesson will quickly run awry if you attempt to do this without creating the environment in which to use it. It's not a stand-alone lesson.

THE *INSIDE* LESSON: A COMPARATIVE ANALYSIS OF TEACHING AND LEARNING

This is such an enjoyable discussion. Students have some pretty kooky ideas about what teaching is! To begin, work on definitions *without* using the term in the definition. Formally present the topic: Teaching versus Learning.

Teaching

The students should first be encouraged to describe what *teaching* looks like. Make sure to establish clearly that they can't use the term in the definition. They might enjoy demonstrating, which is always insightful. Expect at least one student to stand up and pretend to lecture with exaggerated self-importance. Dig into the negativity! Why is *that* considered teaching? Figure out how to dispel it, by your actions and reactions during this discussion and beyond.

Of course, teachers must dispense information in a lecture format sometimes, but *how* we choose to dispense it can certainly vary. Even in lecture format, we can vary presentation and interaction. The students will begin to gain an appreciation for the choices you make as an educator. You won't have to go into pedagogical detail, but they will eventually get the idea that teaching is more than lecturing in your class.

Frankly, it would be much simpler to lecture and tell them what learning is. You could get it over with in ten minutes. However, your transparency in teaching will be reinforced by *not* lecturing and by making sure your students are thinking. Slowly, you'll dissolve their preconceptions of teaching and, eventually, learning.

Learning

Things get a little tricky when they are asked to describe what learning looks like. All too often, students equate the *blah blah blah* of teaching as learning, and you'll find out exactly where they are in this discussion.

Students just seem be at a loss to demonstrate someone *learning*. You might have an artistic sort of student demonstrate by quickly drawing a lightbulb and holding it over his/her head. Or someone might shout "AH HAH!" and follow up by furiously writing on a piece of paper. However, initially, you'll be met with some very blank stares.

This discussion should not be directed by you, but by the students, so if they move off track or run into a wall, don't make statements. Rather, ask questions to get them back on track. The role of facilitator and listener is crucial, and if you convey intellectual curiosity, you will teach by *modeling* learning.

In this type of discussion, the upper-level students will be challenged by the *analysis,* and lower-level students will be challenged by the *concept*.

Many students will be able to share a bit about a memorable lesson a teacher gave them. For example, they might bring up the math teacher who used paper airplanes or the science teacher who had students drop watermelons from the roof. They will need your help in understanding what they experienced as learning, though.

Almost no student will ever indicate that they learn by reading something. Teachers have this ability, which can run us into trouble. Consider that you're learning from this book because you are able to hear and visualize from the words on the page. Low-performing students have to be *taught* these skills.

You're also learning because you have a connection to the material as either a student or a teacher—your immediate connection. These are the skills the students need to understand as *learning*: that tingly feeling of hearing, visualizing, connecting, and applying.

In state assessments, where students have to use critical-thinking skills based solely on reading, this realization really hits home. No matter what subject you teach, the core of *demonstrating* learning is the same: knowing what to do with what you're given, or creating a way to cope with what you're given.

The merits of this discussion are multifaceted. Perhaps, for the first time, students will understand that learning is something they *can do consciously* through asking questions and making connections, but they have ideally reached these conclusions on their own.

Teachers do strive to address these points throughout their lessons, but these brief interactions with the topic don't necessarily reach all students. You don't want the understanding of learning to be the icing on the cake; you want it to be the cake.

We wanted to feel like our teachers cared about the concept or content. It's not, "Those who can't, teach." It's more like "Those who get it, teach it."

We knew Ms. K cared because she would seek us out not only as students but as people. ~ AnnMarie

Additionally, the topic compels students to see teachers from a different perspective. We are not the Great Imparters of knowledge; rather, we are the support systems that help students arrive at knowledge. AnnMarie saw that as me seeking them out as people, which fits because here is where you present that teacher-learner persona in its most organic form: asking questions when students venture their opinions.

You are not the *holder* of the *right* answer. You are the *guide* to the *best* answer. However, students must arrive at it on their own. Some questions you might ask to keep the momentum might include:

Does teaching mean that teachers give you guys the answers?
How do you know when you've learned something?
Should teachers always have the right answer?
If teaching is telling you what you need to know, then why do you think some students say that teachers don't teach them?
Why do you think there's a disagreement between teachers saying that they *did* tell students what they needed to know and students saying, "No, they didn't!"?
Why should we care about the difference between these two concepts?

These are just a few things to think about, and students seem to relish this type of transparent discussion. You can conclude it by saying,

This has been a fantastic discussion, but we do have to stop. (If you hear an "Awwww!" here, you've done an excellent job.) I'm interested in what you've taken away from this topic and our approach to discussion. For homework, please let me know:

- *What insights did you gain from this discussion about teaching and learning?*
- *How do you feel about how we handled this whole-class discussion?*
- *How valuable did you find this lesson to be? (βActively written or prewritten on overhead. Could also be a short handout.)*

Thus endeth the discussion! Thank you!

As a preemptive classroom management measure, this discussion accomplishes several things. First, it clearly puts responsibility for learning in your students' laps, at least for a day. However, you'll have this conversation as a precedent if they start lapsing into their former thinking. You'll have the ability to say, "Remember when we discussed . . . and you said . . . ?"

Many of the discipline issues that teachers encounter directly correlate to this issue of responsibility. However, we tend to be reactive to it, addressing it only negatively and as the need arises. Thus, the students have no connection to the concept of actually taking action to learn. The reactive comments come across as authoritarian or, worse, dictatorial.

"It is *your* responsibility to learn. I'm not going to do your work for you."

Again, stating the obvious gets you nowhere fast. It dribbles out of our mouths almost reflexively, but it's useless and provocative. A Legal Lemur will jump on that observation just for the sake of arguing.

When we address responsibility for learning positively, preemptively, and conceptually, the students have an opportunity to build a foundation for that responsibility in a receptive environment. It is in *that* environment where students learn, and it's really what they desire, even if they don't say so.

Students need to not only come to understand the purpose of their education, but it's also crucial that they're encouraged to come to these conclusions themselves. ~ Daniel

The transition to curriculum is very short, but it is nonetheless a crucial step in the overall process. You've cemented *who* you are and *how* you desire to do things.

Moreover, you've cemented that you have expectations that you know these students have the *ability* to meet. You have gained a modicum of trust and an inkling of respect. They still don't really believe you yet, but they will be ready to move into curriculum. They'll also do so with a greater sense of anticipation and willingness than in their other classes. Your ideal class is born.

Now that the expectations have been set and the students have a clear idea of how the class will function, you'll want to *consistently and purposefully maintain it*, while presenting the curriculum. To *not* do so is a betrayal of the trust and rapport you've previously established and results in many of the discipline issues in secondary classrooms—our focus for the next chapter.

Chapter Eleven

Sticking to Your
Rule and Procedures

THE VOW OF YOUR PERSONA

And then, it happens.

Honeymoon time is over, and the students move into their work. If you haven't had an issue yet, it will emerge when you actually have an assignment for students to complete. Your ability to discipline misbehavior is on the line. Some kid does some *thing* at some point, and you have to *discipline*. No matter how emphatically you've stressed your rule and procedures, it's going to happen.

After all, it's imperative that you maintain control over the classroom at all times. Isn't that on your evaluation thingymawho?

Behavior management is the biggest issue I have. My kids use horrible language and don't see anything wrong with letting the F-word fly during a lesson. Also, at the middle school level, if a teacher turns her back for one second, someone always get injured! Students hit each other, stab each other with pencils, or start physical fights. I would have liked to have had situation training, such as: if your student does this, here are some solutions. ~ Stacey

Stacey brings up the issue that destroys teachers, and at this point in the school year is when you'll see it. However, we can't live in fear of discipline or stress over control. Some instructors are so intent on establishing a control lock that they compete to see who will be the *first* to write a referral for that particular school year, which generally results in a student suspension.

"I was the first to buzz a kid out! Already got a referral!" the self-proclaimed winner will proudly announce in the teacher's lounge, waving a triplicate flag in victory.

How did they know they were first, exactly? Was this information requested by the teacher or simply offered by the dean? In either instance, the whole endeavor is profoundly negative and deeply tragic.

> *I saw it many times with new teachers. They'd start fresh and enthusiastic, looking forward to creating their ideal of what their chosen profession is supposed to be. In nearly every case, that spark was gone inside of a month.*
>
> *Teachers aren't adequately prepared for the reality. At best, they have an idea that gets lost when complications inevitably emerge. However, with the right methods and the right perspective, that ideal class isn't an impossibility. It requires patience, stronger preparation, and adaptability for when things get rough. ~ Daniel*

Make it your goal to never send a student out of the class. Tell students this is your goal when you discuss your Rule:

> You know, guys, I really don't like sending students out of class. No, really! It bugs me to think that you and I can't come up with a solution for something. You can't learn if I send you out, and I believe that most of our issues we can resolve together. This year, it is my goal to not send anyone out of this class.

Note the difference in thinking between "Heh-heh, I was first" and "I believe we can resolve our issues." The message to students is incredibly powerful and clear, but you will have to fight their (relatively justified) skepticism.

> *This is a huge problem in many schools, so I'm glad you have this. The administration is more likely to appropriately penalize a kid if you write fewer referrals, and they want to see that you can deal with issues in your class.*
>
> *Also, schools are perceived differently, based on the number of referrals they have, because those students have less time in the classroom and less time for learning, which then shows in student test scores. ~ Stacey*

Of course, some instances will merit intervention by the dean. However, your goal is to make sure those issues have nothing to do with the class or *you*. Rather, you'll find that most problems result from external social issues, compounded before school, during class changes, or at lunch (e.g., gang fights, bullying, gossip, relationships). Thus, if you must compete, challenge yourself every year with *zero* send-outs, *zero* referrals. Tennis players call that *love*.

PERCEPTIONS OF CONTROL

Effective discipline lies in how you define control, how you convey it, and how willing you are to discipline with an attitude of maturity. It also depends on how seriously you take the vow of your persona, which you've worked so diligently to create!

This discussion might get a little uncomfortable, but it's not intended to malign anyone. Rather, consider the possibility that how we strive to control or discipline students reflects our self-perceptions.

Authentic control is *not* the quick policing of infractions. It is *not* a tight-lipped, hard-nosed, steely-eyed enforcement dictator.

It *is* how you respond when posed with infractions. Every misbehavior is a puzzle that must be solved. *How* you present this solution is in your control. By doing so calmly and logically, you are sticking to the vow of your persona. Control is not *what* you do. It is *how* you do.

I love this distinction because we have a choice in how we deal with kids in the classroom. If I tell the student to stop misbehaving with a smile, what message do I send? However, if I firmly tell the student to stop, and move on with confidence and maturity, it sends a different message. It's all about how you do what you do. ~ *Stacey*

Our thinking lies at the core of every action we make, so if your definition of control is something other than *how you do*, you may run into trouble.

For example, to some teachers, the ability to control equates to how the class perceives them and/or their abilities. The thinking is, "If the class perceives me or my abilities in a positive way, then I have control."

The greatest infraction, then, would be when the student gleefully stomps on that perception. We may overreact. First, we need to determine where our perceptions really are. Consider the following modes of thinking. Which one seems to resonate with you? Be honest!

1. My students listen when I'm talking, and they sit quietly. They respond quickly to my directions. That's when I know I'm in control.
2. When we are enjoying ourselves in the challenge of the assignment, and should issues present, I am calm and assertive—that's when I know I have control.
3. My students love me, and while they do get a little rambunctious, I don't mind. We have a great time! I know I have control when I need it.
4. My students listen when I'm talking, and they sit quietly. They respond quickly to my directions, *and* they love me. That's when I know I'm in control.

Number 1

If this perception of control resonates with you, then you are an authoritarian thinker. What you may really desire is to just have peace and quiet!

(*Note:* Teaching is not a peaceful, quiet job at any grade level prior to college, if even then.)

Number 2

This perception of control conveys an authoritative thinker. Probably, your vision of the ideal class is in line with this thinking. Also, your discipline plan reflects this type of thinking.

Number 3

Permissive thinkers absolutely love their students. They may consider control as a moot point, something to be addressed on as-needed basis.

Number 4

Some teachers want it all: peace and quiet and personal validation from their students. Let's call this authoritarian-plus.

I believe this last type is the type we might be striving for in our ideal classroom. We want the kids to sit and listen to us, and think as we speak. And then, after directions are given, they dive into deep conversations. ~ Stacey

If the teacher is only focused on making his desires happen, obtaining authentic authority will prove to be difficult. If the focus shifts to what's best for the students and how the teacher can get them to learn—as opposed to the focus of maintaining absolute authority or receiving admiration—then the teacher will more naturally find the adaptability to deal with whatever problems arise. ~ Daniel

Probably, you recognize Baumrind's parenting styles here, which have often been applied to teaching styles. Stacey's point is valid—teachers want it all, but is that where we want to be, really? Why? For now, let's consider what messages underlie each of these styles in teaching.

Permissives and authoritarians are quite similar in that they both revolve around how you feel about yourself. The permissive's "C'mon, guys" attitude reflects very low teacher self-esteem because the pleading becomes how the teacher attempts to control.

The messages you send are "Please love me!" and "Please just be good!" That pleading very soon becomes the ineffective, inconsequential white noise of the class. That is, until you lose your control and, out of sheer frustration, "bust out" authoritarian. Students enjoy the sport of moving a permissive to the brink, even though they may like that teacher.

Authoritarians also convey low teacher self-esteem because they have a strange need to be on some sort of credibility pedestal. For them, the concept of teacher and the concept of control are one. It's all about the what (control) and who (me). The logic almost works:

Effective teachers have control in their classrooms.
Thus, control = teacher + teaching.

The premise is valid, but we really need to move into that *how* thinking as opposed to *who* + *what*. We're not quite there yet. We can see that authoritative. Sometimes, we actually reach it; other times, it slides out of our grasp. Why?

One of the reasons we can't hang onto the more desirable perception of control is because in our heart of hearts, we *do* desire authoritarian-plus. Don't you think it would be great to have a classroom full of quiet students who did what you wanted them to do, when you wanted them to do it, *and* loved you? We would feel personally edified and validated as educators, winning all sorts of awards for our well-behaved students . . . mmmm . . . awards . . .

Snap out of it!

It's in this polarity of desiring to be personally edified and desiring complete control that teachers tend to misstep, thinking that they are working the middle ground as it pertains to discipline. However, this mistaken approach is again based on who you are and what you do, not *how*.

The authoritative's perception of control revolves around *how*-thinking. There is no focus on the self-perception of the teacher; rather, the focus is on *how* the class functions. Notice that the goals are completely different as well. Control is *woven* into your thinking as opposed to being the goal.

I don't think it's a conscious decision to be self-centered. Self-esteem may not even enter the teacher's mind. You're right to say that it is usually for the good of the class, but I think that some educators might read this and feel defensive. ~ Stacey

But, the teacher who can focus on how to promote learning instead of maintaining his position can react to disciplinary issues with the lesson in mind and handle things more effectively. ~ Daniel

It's interesting that a teacher's discipline plan is usually geared to the desirable authoritative style. On paper, we look *good*—perfectly composed and calm. All is for the good of the class, we tell ourselves.

But if our *thinking* is not truly and consciously authoritative, then our gut reaction to that very first tittle of misbehavior, that first jot of attitude, despite all of our authoritative planning and forethought, is generally going to be either permissive or authoritarian. We'll go anywhere but where we wanted to go because we did not truly ingest the authoritative perception of control.

You can avoid breaking your vow by making the connection to the authoritative philosophy of *how I do is my control*. You've got a lot to process in nanoseconds, so it's helpful to stay positive.

First up: What does the *intent* of the misbehaving student(s) seem to be?

Consider this example:

David plays on the football team, and he begins to roughhouse with another student. There is no sense of maliciousness in their behavior, but it is not conducive to starting the class. You're also concerned that it may escalate.

You make the choice to stop the silliness. *How* you stop the silliness is your ability to control.

> TEACHER: *(moves to proximity and sightline of student, clear voice, calm, direct)* David . . . ?
>
> DAVID: Yeah? *(laughing, still kind of play-slapping the other student, who is responding likewise)*
>
> TEACHER: *(calm and assertive)* David. George. *(The teacher indicates desk/chairs with a nod of the head, eyebrows raised, and a slight smile.)*

This is your first line of action: passive *presumption* based on observation.

This teacher has given David and George the benefit of the doubt that their intent is nonmalicious, based on her observation. How the teacher responded conveyed that benefit of the doubt: *calm, assertive, eyebrows, smile, and subtle indication.*

Do you see how the teacher has conveyed the expectation of what she wants the students to do (stop the behavior), but also a sense of "I have every confidence that you know what the right thing is to do"? The teacher could have said, "Cupcakes and applesauce," but *what* she said did not matter. *How* it was said and *how* it was conveyed made the difference. That's positive, authentic control.

The onus for conditioning for positivity as it pertains to discipline is, unsurprisingly, on the teacher. Moreover, we're also deconditioning students (and ourselves) from the usual flow of consequences-driven discipline.

"Why should we bother?" some teachers may posit. "Don't we have *enough* to do, for cryin' out loud?"

Well, we're not asking you to do *more*. We're asking you to do *differently*. This type of control is the most beneficial in establishing a positive environment because conditioning requires patience and consistency.

And the naysayers' chorus is "Those students'll walk all over you if you don't show them who's in control."

That's just it! If you are truly in control, you will not have to *show* them. It will be infused in the fabric of the class.

> *I definitely had a few teachers who were soft-spoken and let all the students walk over them. I don't think it's right, but kids are mean. Those teachers would submit and let the students run the class instead. And it was the last year they were my teachers as well. The teacher needed to take control, but alas, just never did.*
>
> *I prefer a stern teacher who can joke around and have fun days, but also be serious. I want a teacher that will talk to me, not talk at me. ~ Linda Allan*

What Linda has asked for is simply this: a mature adult, who responds in a calm, mature way.

But kids do not know how to deal or respond to a teacher who reacts in a calm, mature way. I'm thinking this depends on the students' cultures. For example, how are they disciplined at home? Some kids only know how to respond to rude, mean, and nasty . . . they can't handle themselves with calm and mature reactions. ~ Stacey

What someone is familiar with does come into play, but teenagers are social beings who respond to the pressure to conform. If the teacher responds calmly, and the student goes verbally haywire, then that student will soon feel the sting of performing solo, without backup. And, he or she will usually stop. If you are fair, calm, and clear, and stick to your persona, other students will create the pressure for appropriate response.

We also have to ask the question, what do we mean by "respond to a teacher"? As it pertains to procedures and rules, does response mean *compliance* or something else? Compliance isn't the goal—*understanding* is.

STUDENTS FORGETTING PROCEDURES

When a student forgets to follow a procedure, one of two things will probably happen. Either another student will remind him/her about the procedure, or the class will wait and watch your response. They are observing your consistency: *How will she react? Will he yell? Will she get mad?*

How you react to a lapse in procedures is a test in patience and resolve, absolutely, and if you're going to break your vow, it will probably be here. But your promise is that there will be no consequences for forgetting a procedure. Thus, you have to stick to that vow—even if it means biting your tongue and hiding frustration.

If you use "benefit of the doubt" thinking for procedures, coupled with waiting for the student to actually do it, then you have made your point. You have the control. Remember our sharpening-pencil scenario? Let's work it through, in stages.

You've used the Hand to get the class's attention, and as the class quiets down, some kid starts sharpening his pencil. *VVVVWHIRRRR-chackchack-VVVVWHIR.*

He stops as he realizes that you've started, but he looks at you and doesn't move. What do you do? It's a standoff.

It's no longer an appropriate time to use the pencil sharpener, so how do you remind him about this procedure? It would be so much easier to say, "Go ahead, we'll wait." However, if you do that, you've broken your vow to your procedure, and you'd probably be sarcastic anyway.

Another knee-jerk response might be, "Can't you see I've put my hand up? What's the procedure, kid?"

In this reaction, you've broken the vow of your persona. Plus, you've embarrassed the student. How can you get your message across without too much ado? Keep it on PAR!

Tier 1 Response: Passively Presumptive (P)

To stick to your vow, think about how you'd react to an adult doing the same thing. Probably, you'd make eye contact, smile in acknowledgment, and just keep right on talking, *making the presumption that the adult will realize the error and handle it accordingly.*

Give the student the opportunity to make the best decision. More than likely, he/she will stop sharpening and move on to Plan B. Situation resolved. Everyone's dignity is intact.

However, let's say the student smiles and just keeps right on sharpening. You then need to bump up your game. The following scenarios adapt strategies from Fay and Funk's *Teaching with Love and Logic*, and this author highly recommends this resource!

Tier 2 Response: Actively Presumptive (A)

TEACHER: James? *(smiling warmly, indicates student's seat with a head motion)*

You still convey hope through your response the student gets that he's doing something disruptive, but you give him a little verbal nudge in the right direction. However, he may respond with the ultimate ignition for teacher frustration (and the source of most grey hair):

STUDENT: What? *(with cherubic innocence and just a dash of chip-on-the-shoulder)*

You have an option to be a smart-aleck yourself at this point, and it would probably taste pretty good. Rolling your eyes is a natural response. Sighing as if you can't buh-lieve this kid is so clueless. You could choose the sarcastic and condescending route, but it will only serve to make things worse. Bite your tongue. You're a professional after all. You are a how-thinker!

TEACHER: *(smiles, whispers)* I've started, so . . .

This is the approach I take because it allows the student to think through what is happening right now and what the next choice they need to make is. . . . However, now that he has said something silly, chances are the rest of my class

*has gotten sidetracked with either giggling or started side conversations. Now,
what? ~ Stacey*

If your class goes sideways, your instinct might be to become a police of-
ficer: "Alright, nothing to see here. Let's move along."

Don't do that. There actually is something to see—*you*, sticking to your
own promise! Either use the procedure for quieting the class (if the sidetrack
merits) or consider another tactic.

To Hand or Not to Hand?

Using the Hand to regroup the class at this point may or may not work to
offset the distraction of a student being funny. The Law of Classroom Humor
says that anything a fellow student says is automatically more interesting than
what you have to say. Thus, you have to gauge the noise level.

You'll probably have a good idea of where the class's highest noise level
is if you've done some of the previous activities, such as the icebreaker. A
consideration for use of the Hand in this situation would be if the noise level
is more than 50 percent of that highest noise level.

If you're under 50 percent, consider an alternative for getting the class back
on track. Sometimes, a quirky catchphrase is all you need:

*Your legacy continues because, till this day, I still use "But we digress . . ." I
share the story about how my passionate drama teacher would use this phrase
when the class would deviate from whatever the focus was. ~ Masac Dorlouis*

Maybe because the word *digress* is generally unknown to students this age
or because it sounds kind of funny, it may do the trick for you. Another
possibility is *divagate*. When you use a pompous, official-sounding accent
along with your phrase, you'll catch their attention and get everyone back
on track.

Tier 3 Response: Revel in a Teachable Moment of a
Class of One (R)

But, let's say the student is hell-bent on pushing the situation into an issue.
Moving from cherubic and cute, he then becomes indignant.

STUDENT: What!!??? *(with hands out, pleading, more indignant, more
chippish-ish)*

Okay! You've given him the benefit of the doubt. You've given him a "hint,"
and now you need to remind him about the procedure explicitly.

Is it frustrating? Absolutely. Does it not drive you crazy that the student seems to be exhibiting a lack of common sense? Certainly. Welcome to the adolescent mindset and that squiggly line between your eyebrows.

Nonetheless, keep in mind that you are always dually teaching: teaching the content of your course (the inside) and teaching students how to be mature adults (the outside). As much as possible, you'll teach maturity implicitly, but sometimes, you're going to have to explicitly address it.

Here's where it gets fiddly though. If you step slightly off into even the *potential* for sarcasm or humiliation, peppered with an attitude of "You stupid kid, you" you're asking for trouble. Thus, if you treat the moment as *teachable*, you'll be in better shape.

> TEACHER: *(whispering warmly and with encouragement)* I've already started the class, so now is not a good time to sharpen your pencil. Remember the procedure is to only sharpen when it's appropriate. You can borrow one from up front until it's a better time. Probably, I'll be done in about ten minutes. *(Conclude with a smile; go back to front of class.)*

From here the student only has one place to go, really, unless he wants to move into outright disrespect. You, as a teacher, have moved through a sequence of responses, all of which were delivered in a positive way. Total time, from start to finish on this PAR, was about twenty seconds.

If the student chooses to be a jerk from this point on, then we're moving into "rule" territory: he's being disrespectful. Plus, ten bucks and a latte say the whole class has become silent anyway to try and hear what you've just whispered.

For those of you who love the warning systems, consider these three tiers as three progressively stronger warnings, but note that they are neither presented nor delivered as such. Moreover, depending on the severity of the student's response (for example, a jump to smart-alecky), you might move directly to a whisper. Because you haven't limited yourself, you have the option to choose how to respond appropriately.

You may also be a "check mark" person—fine. Consider these three tiers to be three *mental* check marks on a *mental* tally sheet, but note that each check mark indents a bit deeper.

I BROKE THE RULE, AND I LIKED IT

If a student breaks the rule, on any level, the other students literally hold their breath. The silence when someone steps over the line is heavy. That's one of the ways you can determine that it's time to dole out consequences: the students are silent.

However, to ensure that you are staying true to your vow, your consequences must be logical. *Escalating* or *snowball* misbehavior is usually a little harder to deal with than *isolated* misbehavior because teachers lose steam as the issue grows. Likewise, students can wear us down with repetitive *dripping-water torture* behavior because it's the same thing over and over. Let's see what happens when James moves into rule-breaking territory:

> STUDENT: Jeez, I'm just sharpening my pencil. How am I supposed to do my work? You teachers are always on my back . . . *(something along these lines).*

Take a breath. Always take a cleansing breath. Wisdom waits. Maturity tilts its head to the side and wonders like a curious puppy. You are now moving into concerned mode over this *snowball* behavior.

You should be concerned that the student is responding to you in this way. It signals something is going on. More than likely, it is not you because you have been professional, warm, and encouraging.

However, something you said may have been misconstrued. Thus, taking the time to talk to this student is warranted.

Tier 1 Response: Concern

> TEACHER: *(slightly frowning with concern, whispers)* Would you come outside with me for a minute, James? *(TEACHER goes to the door, does not look back, goes outside, and holds door expectantly.)*

It's important to note the whispering and sense of expectation. That sense of expectation is the last presumption we can make. The whispering is respectful.

> *This makes the rest of the students wonder, "How bad is James going to get it?" It provokes a sense of curiosity while also letting the student know the teacher means business.* ~ Christina

Yes, this has stopped the class's momentum for those of you keeping track. You purposefully haven't gone back to your lesson. This lesson in discipline is just as important, if not more so. Not only is it a lesson to the individual student, but it is also a lesson to the class: "I will stick to my persona and my vow, no matter what. I will not lower my expectations of you or myself."

I love the concept of stepping outside. Without an audience of supporters, a lot of students lose their edge. It's one-on-one direct language that hopefully puts the student in a safe place. ~ Crystal

Once outside, your best strategy is still concern, mixed with surprise.

TEACHER: What's up, James? You okay?

You give the student that one final opportunity to somehow justify and apologize for his behavior. Maybe he's had a bad day. *Wait for it*. Count to twenty. Do not lecture. Find out what is really wrong. Usually, it will have to do with something else entirely, a breakup, a headache, etc. The student, when approached calmly and with concern, will most likely apologize immediately.

From there, emphasize that you're glad he is okay. With very few, if any, exceptions, he will return to the class, complete the consequence of being singled out and addressed outside, and the class will move on.

However, if you still get silence from the student, then you'll want to invoke the muse of confident admonition.

Tier 2 Response: Admonition

Reprimanding a high school or middle school student should never be done in front of the class. To the best of your ability, do it to the side or outside. You'll find that you are able to address the situation more calmly. This author has made the unfortunate mistake of admonishing a student in front of the class. Here were the results:

Not everything in the class was sunshine and rainbows. I remember being on the receiving end of a consequence. I was playing around with another student, and I had a pencil. Not thinking about it, I pointed the other sharp end toward the student's face, and Ms. Keller saw that.

She yelled at me for doing it pretty harshly in front of the entire class. Even though I was playing around, I could have hurt the other student. I was a really sensitive teenager though, and I remember feeling about as low as one could be and really embarrassed. It took me awhile to get over feeling like that. ~ Tori

In retrospect, although some may find the reaction justified, given the potential for physical danger, I should *never* have admonished her publically. Should I have noted to Tori that what she was doing was potentially harmful? Absolutely! And I knew Tori's intent was definitely not malicious! Thus, I overreacted.

It is okay to apologize to a student when you are in the wrong, and it may even help build the relationship. ~ Stacey

To finalize the scenario with James, you'll want to speak honestly and sincerely. Identify the issue and why it was an issue:

TEACHER: James, I'm sure you didn't intend to be disrespectful, but when you respond to my requests to stop in an argumentative way, we run into trouble. *(pause)* We're okay, James, I just wanted to make sure you were okay. Thanks. *(TEACHER smiles when STUDENT acknowledges the issue nonverbally or verbally.)*

OUTRIGHT DISRESPECT

There's power in a request that doesn't exist in a command because you compel the student to *decide* what to do. Make "requests" when dealing with a rule break. If you make a request as opposed to giving an order, the student must choose. For example:

Request: Angela, will you come outside with me please?
Order: Angela . . . outside . . . now.

If you use a request, only then you can *softly* and with great concern ask, "Are you refusing to do as I've asked?"

It's a dilemma for the student! She will have to acknowledge that, indeed, she is *refusing* to do something that you've politely, professionally, warmly, calmly, logically asked her to do. What you've done is taken the wind out of her little teenage sails. If the teacher has a completely professional and, indeed, completely respectful attitude, the student has a more difficult time justifying a snotty refusal.

It's so much easier to refuse someone who says:

"What do you think you're doing? Get outside; I want to talk to you right now."

than it is to refuse someone who says:

"Janice, would you mind stepping outside with me for a moment? I'd like us to talk for a minute."

Even so, you may still get this response: "Yeah, I refuse. Whatcha gonna do?"

That's a hard-core kid. More than likely, one of the all-stars you've noted, so you shouldn't be greatly surprised. However, calmly, and with great disappointment tinged with surprise (whether you actually feel it or not) in your voice, say, "I see. I was hoping we could resolve this together."

It's the concern, disappointment, and surprise that *deescalates* the situation usually. Then, quietly take your action. Don't tell the student what you're going to do. You don't have to. Just . . . go do it. Telling them what you're going to do only feeds the disruption.

Here's the clincher though: unless the behavior was sudden and violent, you must have given it a shot with the student. You can't jump to action without giving the student the opportunity to make amends.

Depending on the severity of the infraction, you might send the student out of class, make an immediate telephone call to a parent, or send an e-mail later. It really depends on what the student has done.

We all know what to do if a fight breaks out or a student is threatening someone, but coping with disrespect is where we and the students need the clarification. Thus, if your student refuses to work through the problem with you, think about the best, most effective recourse you can take: parental contact, administrative intervention, talking to a coach/sponsor. Does the refusal merit being removed from class? Why or why not? If it doesn't merit removal, then consider where the issue really lies and follow through as best you can.

What's imperative to understand is that you do not have to follow a sequence as dictated by any sort of discipline plan. You can, for example, jump to admonition, if the situation merits admonition. Tori's example, where there was the potential for injury, merited admonition, just not *public* admonition. However, she was a mature student, and this teacher should have used concern first. *I'm sorry, Tori! ~ Ms. K.*

You may run into a wall of disrespect in a student, which is usually indicative of a larger emotional or psychological issue. More than likely, you'll feel this issue well before you have a standoff. (As soon as you recognize that feeling, it's worth taking a look into the student's records and talking to the counselor.)

It's important that you follow your own plan first, followed by the necessary due diligence for your school. That is about the only way you'll be able to sleep at night without falling into despair—knowing that you have warmly, professionally, and kindly worked with this student.

I had one student who I feel like I could write an entire book on. Here's what it comes down to: building the relationship. However, with this one particular student, I tried and tried and tried some more to build a relationship and figure out what was really going on with him. I called home, had mom and dad come in for a conference, spoke with guidance and spoke with my reading coach. He was immature, and the misbehavior was for attention.

I tried giving him positive attention . . . didn't work . . . he got all of the negative attention. Throughout the year, he was sent to time-out at least twice a week, given detentions, referrals, ISS, OSS. He called me a "raggedy roach" and was then suspended at the end of the year for threatening to bring a gun to school to shoot me.

The question arises, are there some kids where nothing works? Should admin have transferred him to the other reading teacher's class to see if that was a better fit? What else could we as teachers and as a school done for this child? Not every kid is a fit for public, mainstream classrooms, and not all children want to learn. ~ Stacey

Stacey went well above and beyond where most educators would go. If nothing else, this kid will remember that one teacher cared enough to try. However, Stacey didn't give up, and she can prove that with her follow-ups. No one will ever say that she didn't do everything she *could*, and that's all that can be done.

ACTIVE OFFENSE VERSUS REACTIVE DEFENSE

One should strive, even in the face of outright disrespect, never to lose a sense of humor. With it, you'll be able to maintain your calm and stay on the offense. In order to achieve that, however, teachers need to avoid indulging in a defensive posture.

When I was teaching contrast transitions, I was using sound effects to highlight the turnaround thinking in terms such as: *but*, *however*, and *on the other hand*.

Each time we came across a transition in the reading, I would make a bell noise: *DING DING!* I did this a few times, with some students dinging along with me, until one young man got the bright idea to say:

"I got your ding-ding right here, b—."

He said this quite low, so only a few students heard it. Now, this was outright disrespect, no buts about it. (Nod to seating charts, he had been flagged as a potentially troublesome student, given his discipline record. Thus, he sat right in front of me. Imagine the disruption had he been sitting farther away!)

I had a hard time not smiling at this because the young man's last name was easily connected to the concept of a bell. Thus, the "ding-ding" just struck me as incredibly funny.

I chuckled inwardly. After finishing my thought on the current lesson, I asked the class to excuse me. The student was removed, and a referral followed. The student didn't argue with my choice because he knew he had crossed the line.

However, I didn't yell at him, nor did I lose my cool. Because I allowed for that humor, I had the patience to cope with the situation in the most effective way. Additionally, the entire class did not suffer from the result of one student's side step.

When the student returned the next day, he was greeted *tabula rasa*. I confirmed that he understood why I wrote a referral, and he agreed he had stepped over the line, apologizing. We moved on, with no further walls between us.

I like that you have this here. It shows that we don't forget about the situation, don't ignore what happened but return to it the next day in a calm, respectful way! Love it! ~ Stacey

Each day with the students should be a new slate, but so many teachers do not or cannot do this. The problem with teachers treating a "problem" student differently after a situation is that the student then feels like an outsider and will act accordingly, perpetuating a cycle. If the student isn't given a fresh slate after an altercation/disruption, what's the point of not creating another situation in the classroom? ~ Christina

Now, let's consider how this event might have played out with a snap, reactive defensive posture. This teacher, with much righteous indignation, might say: "Young man, that is not the way you speak to me. I am your teacher, and you will respect me. You apologize right this minute, or I'm sending you out!"

This phrasing is general, but probably, you've used something along these lines at some point (I did!). However, in analysis, the condescension, the dictatorial consequence, and the very weak, self-edifying nature of stating your *position* in the class (as if reminding the student that you are the teacher, duh, makes any difference) all speak to one thing: you have a chip on your shoulder.

You feel absolutely justified in reacting with harshness and say, "I only have a chip on my shoulder because these rude kids drive me to say things like that."

Cash in that chip.

Reacting or acting defensively is the weakest posture to take in the mind of the adolescent. It's weak because they're immune to it. What throws them for a loop, however, is someone who doesn't react as expected, and especially if that someone seeks to understand their position in whatever issue is at stake. Revel in that moment. If there's humor, see it.

Teachers also tend to harbor resentment, which is a large component of that chip. Rather than harbor resentment, consider the lifeline you've already established with parents. You've met them (hopefully), and now you can work together to find the root of the issue. Go on the offense, not the defense.

Usually, the student's issue has nothing to do with the teacher, but other things going on in his/her life. Thus, the teacher can determine if the counselor should be brought into the situation or not.

There are no cut-and-dry consequences or strategies for discipline. All that can be controlled is how you react and present those consequences. The underlying message should be: "My teacher is fair, and she cares about me."

It's also important to note that because you will send so few students out of your class, *when you do have a problem*, the response from administration will probably be more effective and supportive.

Whose class is an administrator likely to head to first? Mr. C's class, the teacher who hasn't buzzed a student out all year (likely conclusion—this is a substantial disciplinary issue), or Ms. B's class, the teacher who buzzes a kid out every day?

Being a teacher does not just mean that you're presenting your state's standards and benchmarks. It's showing students what's socially acceptable, how to live, how to ask questions, and how to be a better person. ~ AnnMarie

THE JOY OF WATCHING
A TEACHER LOSE IT: CYBERBAITING

It's a sight that all students seem to enjoy: the day the teacher completely loses his/her cool and yells, cries, or otherwise goes off the deep end. Do the students remember these moments? Oh, yes.

I still talk with classmates about one of our former teachers who absolutely lost it in the classroom—ripped posters off of the wall with a yardstick, slapped each and every one of our desks with said yardstick and yelled for about fifteen minutes straight before storming out of the class. Although I learned a lot in that class, that particular day is the only thing I truly remember about that teacher, and it's the only thing I associate with that class. ~ Christina

This teacher was lucky enough to escape the horrors of going viral with the behavior. Today's students have the advantage of technology and social networks. Consider whether or not your students are baiting you to lose your temper so that they can bask in their fifteen minutes of web fame.

Some students do their best to bring the teacher to that point in an effort to avoid doing work or being, at least for a moment, in control. It's a skill, really—an identification of what really ticks a teacher off. By pressing that button enough times, the student might score a good cry or perhaps a red face, screaming in anger. Five hundred bonus points for teacher profanity!

Teachers seem to lose it when they feel personally threatened. It may be masked as professionalism: "The student is disrupting the entire class!" However, most of the disruptive behavior that drives teachers crazy is what occurs when they are speaking or trying to speak. Thus, the freaking out really has more to do with perceived loss of power. It would be more accurate to say, "The student is disrupting me!"

Never fall into the pit of despair that you are somehow powerless. You are not. Even if you have to say it as a mantra to yourself, do it until you believe it. It's a confidence that you need to wear and project: *I am not powerless.*

The awareness of the cyberbaiting sport may be enough to help you spot potential players in the game. These will be individual baiters, insulting you. You may also be victim of a group bait. That is, several students engage in disrespectful badgering (aka "trolling"), mockery, or belligerence.

What's important to notice is that a baiting situation in the classroom has an air of suspense on top of the shenanigans. Those who are actually recording, as well as those who are in the vicinity of the recording device, will be quieter or speak quickly and wait, looking at each other as though sharing a private joke. They can't help looking surreptitiously at the device because this is their most comfortable domain.

Position yourself in that pocket and become still and silent. Take paper with you and write down all of those who seemed to be part of the issue. Reflect on who possibly started the game. If you are too shaken up to write, then draw a diagram, whatever will calm you down and at least help you look like you haven't gone over the edge.

Consider also that once you've identified the starting point, you may have a better chance at changing the behavior. What you may also find is that the primary student has some sort of emotional and/or learning disability.

Your goal is to make sure you understand that the students' behavior does not impact you. You are the professional. If they're laughing, that's okay. They're not professionals. They'll stop, eventually. Listen to them. Write down their comments for later use. You'd be surprised at how quickly they stop baiting when they realize you're writing down what they say.

Silence works. It's scary to them because they don't know what you're thinking about doing. They are accustomed to adults just letting go.

Additionally, be on the lookout for the student holding the cell phone. If you see that you're being recorded, consider using proximity to stop it. More than likely, your school has a policy about cell phones, so know when and if you are permitted to take the phone. You might also want to check whether it's within your rights to delete any recordings made of you, once the phone is in your possession. E-mail or call the parents as soon as possible.

Another course of action to consider would take a bit more planning. Know who has what planning period at any given time. You and your peers can have an agreement to "cover" each other in the event of a meltdown. Thus, if you find yourself standing on the verge, you can step outside and ask your on-call buddy to take over until you are back to rights.

All of us will have at least one experience where we need a few minutes to regroup. Don't be embarrassed about that. Plan for it. Own it. The knowledge that you have a plan should help you out with that stress.

REACHING OUT TO STUDENTS
WHEN YOU'RE FRUSTRATED

One of the advantages of working with adolescents is that they do possess the ability to reason—whether they opt to use that ability or not is another thing. If you find that you are at your wit's end, and you've tried other strategies, consider asking the students what they think.

I remember you being quite upset and that you came to me (of all people). I think we talked of patience, control, and simply letting things go, or not letting things get to you, as well as the purpose behind some of the problems you'd encountered.

As I mentioned before, many hopeful teachers seeking their ideal class get crushed by the daily reality of coping with discipline. You almost headed that route, but you chose to fight it instead. I remember you still stumbled upon the way occasionally, but those first few years were those years where you were a work-in-progress, trying out different things to find your way.

I think that's probably what was most admirable about you as a teacher— not that you were perfect, or that you easily grasped these concepts you write about—but you were willing to find them on your own, despite the enormous pressure from students as well as the heavy constraints of the administration.

Most enthusiastic new teachers are like those who have their faith harshly tested. Some fall, give up, or give in. They choose the standardized monotony because it's the easy way out. You chose to face that challenge. You chose to grow and innovate. You chose to persevere no matter how difficult the conditions.

To me, that choice to persevere is worth the highest level of respect and admiration as a teacher and a human being. The funniest, most ironic and delightful part, is that when you were at your darkest, when your faith in your job was at its weakest, of all things you could have done, you came to your students.

What a perfect picture for this book. ~ Daniel

In one of my field-experience classrooms, the kids were crazy rambunctious and nothing seemed to work. So I asked, during a calm and clear time, what I could do to let them know when things were getting out of hand. One student quite seriously said, "Mrs. D, just say 'Yo, this is whack.'"

I thought this was the craziest suggestion ever. But the next day, the kids were really just not into having a discussion. Not with me, anyway. So I waited for a lull in the laughs and said, quite loudly, "Yo, this is whack."

And what do you know, they all turned to look at me and closed their mouths. The kid whose suggestion it was said, "Hey, ya'll, she know what it be. Let's get with it." And the rest of the lesson went incredibly well!

Sometimes, just knowing how to talk to the class on their level, or how to get their attention for that quick moment to get your foot in the door, is all it takes to redirect behavior. And if the class has a hand in how to do this, well, even better. ~ AnnMarie

YOUR EMOTIONAL AWARENESS

Students seem to appreciate an emotionally aware teacher who can express emotions without forcing them on anyone or the class. Because emotions are personal, their expression should be personal. Thus, when you are aware of how you're feeling and use that awareness to foster your dual purpose for teaching, you'll give a powerful lesson in maturity. The message received is: "My teacher does have emotions, but he/she handles them. They don't control him/her."

Consider also that if you are truly depressed, sad, angry at the start of a class, it's helpful to tell the students this information, providing only necessary details. For example, you might tell your incoming class: "Okay, I'm a little freaked out! Please let me know if I'm saying or doing anything out of line. I don't want to take it out on you."

No specifics, mind you. The more general, the better. Otherwise, you run the risk of divulging information you shouldn't. A simple, "I'm just stressed. Don't wanna go into it," should suffice.

There is an implied trust in sharing emotions. If you can't share the actual reason why you are frustrated or upset, then acknowledge it: "Guys, I don't know what's wrong with me, today. I'm a mess. I'm going to try to figure it out, so don't let me take it out on you. Let me know if I'm being weird or something."

Wouldn't you rather that sharing and trust to be preemptive and in your control?

The effective teacher will have a classroom that is free of hostility, and this begins with the teacher. Ms. Keller exhibited this characteristic by being firm, fair, and interactive. We knew the rules up front, but positive bantering and discussion was always modeled by her. However, testing the limits of propriety was rare. For the times when a student did get rude, she was quick to point it out.

I think that being up front and open about these instances helps to quell future occurrences. It is a constant balance-beam routine to maintain this classroom environment. Obviously, there are "off days" for students and teachers. There was the occasional script thrown or screaming fit, but Ms. Keller did make amends, and she did explain why she felt the way she did (once calm, of course).

The balance beam involves a good rapport with your students, a good dia-logue between classroom and leader, because it's a give-and-take. When the teacher models acceptable behavior, including positive criticism or how to re-ject ideas in a respectful manner or even joke respectfully, the classroom tends to run more smoothly. ~ AnnMarie

While we all know that we are models for students, are we doing it? Are we modeling maturity, patience, consistency, emotional awareness, control, and authentic power? Think about the last time you "lost it" in the classroom. Some possibilities for what caused it might be:

—snowball behavior (starts small and grows)
—water-torture behavior (constant flow of repetitive small stuff)
—outright disrespect
—student sport
—perception of powerlessness
—lack of emotional self-awareness

Which one seems to be the most prevalent culprit for you? Being able to identify it will help you create coping mechanisms.

Practice *doing* this:

Saying a student's name calmly, professionally, and with meaning.
Raising your eyebrows meaningfully.
Smiling a small, warm, professional smile.
Using appropriate body language to send a message.

Practice *saying* this:

"Are you refusing to do as I have asked?"

Practice *thinking* this:

How I do is in my control.
I am not powerless.
With a little practice, these strategies will become second nature to you.

How you model maturity and decision-making truly counts. When we respond appropriately and consistently to any issue that may arise, the responses from the students tend to match that. It may not (most likely will not) happen in the beginning, but consistent fairness and respect, and sticking to your vow, will win out in the end.

Unfortunately, so many teachers don't see the students sitting in their classrooms day after day as people. They don't take the time out to help them grow and learn about themselves, their responsibilities, and how what they're learning actually does fit in to the grand scheme of things. Experiencing the real-world connection helps make the concepts you are trying to teach a little more comprehendible. While these strategies may eventually become second nature, it does take time to get there! Stick to it, for yourself and for your students.

Some students don't care about rules. But when you establish a rapport of mutual respect, and they know that you care about them as people, you can usually manage anything that comes up. It's actually helpful at times when you have students who are disrespectful or break the rules because it's a good teaching opportunity. If you're constantly buzzing students out, the class doesn't get the benefit of seeing how to handle conflict in the real world—a valuable life lesson.

After all, it's good citizens we're looking to build—not mindless robots capable of taking a test, but incapable of living and interacting with others. ~ AnnMarie

Chapter Twelve

A Class of Thinkers: Socrates in Action

AnnMarie's point about mindless robots speaks to the core of what we want most from our public school system: good citizens and critical thinkers.

Again, we sat in a circle and began. We ate lunch together and still went back and forth on our impressions. This was how learning should be. Ideas clicked in my mind; I felt connected to each one of my classmates and Ms. K. When we left, we were still discussing the book! ~ Crystal

I have had several teachers that I felt were good teachers (you being one of them). For me the important thing to teach is "why," not just the solution. If you can teach someone why, then he or she can figure out the solution. Not only that, but they can take what they have learned and apply it to other instances that may not be exactly the same. ~ Zach Russakis

Feeling connected . . . teaching the why . . . applications of learning. These are phrases that we want to hear fall out of our students' mouths! So, how can we get there? One way is take a look down the road you *don't* want to travel.

NO MORE QUESTIONS

I had the opportunity to observe several teachers' classrooms, and one particular teacher was having a really tough time. The students were interrupting him for all sorts of procedural things (going to the bathroom, going to their lockers) and general, water-drip-torture silly behavior. His goal and lesson was to get them to discuss a short story they had (ostensibly) read for homework.

After handling adolescent-proclaimed emergencies for about fifteen minutes, the teacher was a tad stressed. However, he dutifully took attendance, which took another few minutes. Then, he had to demonstrate that he could teach, especially with a guest in the room. So, after a mercifully short version of *What Page, Huh?* he asked a question along the lines of "Why does this character make these choices?"

We finally got started with that sharp, analytical question. A few students raised their hands, and others shouted out responses, both on and off topic. However, the teacher only responded to the student who had shouted out something silly because that interruption made the whole class laugh. So, he tried the question again.

He got some sort of answer from another student, and because it was the correct answer, and he'd lost so much time on off-task things (twenty-five minutes out of a fifty-minute class period), he decided they would write paragraphs instead. Frustrated, he said, "Well, since we can't have a polite discussion, then you'll just have to write it out."

The class's response to the work-punishment was negative, of course. He turned his back to write on the chalkboard, which led to more misbehavior, including a few choice expletives and the slamming of textbooks. While he was trying to write the questions, one young lady asked a legitimate question about the story. He tersely replied, "Don't ask me any more questions. Just write your paragraph."

Don't ask me any more questions.

That experience really stuck with me. Don't ask questions? What the heck was that all about? Isn't that what students are supposed to do?

The research is already in that collaboration increases learning. However, the collaborative nature of questions is lost when teachers block the questioning process or are the only ones asking the questions. What about the collaborative nature of questioning as a necessary step towards critical-thinking skills?

If an inquiring mind is the basis for the pursuit and the advancement of knowledge, then inspiring a student to ask questions is a fundamental part of teaching.
~ Daniel

QUESTIONS AND CRITICAL THINKING

Are teachers truly drawing out student questions? Our gut reaction might be, "Of course I make sure I answer all of their questions! Students just don't really ask too many. Besides, it's their job to *answer* the questions to demonstrate they've learned."

Is it?

Is the start of learning *answering* the questions or *asking* them? How many times have you asked your students questions versus the number of times they have asked you?

Naysayers may interject, "Well. Pffft. They have to learn to find their own answers." That would be just fine, *if* the students had any idea of how to ask questions properly.

Recently, I went with my son to his university admissions office. I was determined not to intervene with his dealings with the counselor. I was determined that he would do this on his own, and I would only observe.

What I found was that my son *responded* well to questions posed to him by the counselor. He also actively *listened* to the counselor. However, my proudest moment was *when he asked for clarification* on a matter concerning his program choice. That effort impressed me more because, in asking a question, he had to be vulnerable for a moment.

Do we unconsciously condition students to *avoid* asking questions, yet be prepared to answer them? Is there some pride issue or myth that we can dispel with the asking of questions?

Adults, in general, seem to have fewer qualms about asking questions. They've experienced firsthand what happens when they should have (but didn't) ask a question for clarification. (Experience sure wins out after you've had your utilities shut off.) However, adolescents just don't have that experience as a foundation.

Let's consider how we might possibly be contributing to the problem. If teachers envision an ideal class as students quietly doing their work, then those teachers are not encouraging questions and, unconsciously or potentially, they are not encouraging *learning*. Of course, they may inquire: "Does anyone have any questions?"

But this perfunctory catchall question, even *if* asked with the best of intentions, does not *encourage* questioning. It sends a completely different message—"Did any of you *not* understand what I just said?"

For high schoolers, there is some squirrelliness about asking questions anyway, never mind answering them. Of course, no one wants to ask "stupid" questions. No matter how much teachers try to instill the value of questions with the adage, "There are no stupid questions," the teacher's impatience with questions may show through facial expression and body language.

I was so nervous to answer questions in class! However, I definitely felt more comfortable asking them when the teacher had made it abundantly clear that questions were okay. A lot of the "question asking" for students is based on how comfortable they feel with the teacher. If the teacher is open and willing to answer, the students are open and willing to ask. ~ Christina

How, exactly, are we doing in the question department? Do we encourage questions, or do we throw out perfunctory attempts at garnering questions? Do we see the act of acquiring questions as a necessary evil or as a genuinely interesting endeavor?

It may be that we become impatient, mostly because we thought that what we just said was clear *enough*. We thought that a first-grader would have understood what we just said, it was so crystal clear. We thought . . . we thought . . .

If your students aren't asking questions, it isn't because you've done a bang-up job in your explanation. It may because of their pride, fear, shyness, nervousness, unwillingness, or apathy, but it isn't because of your flawless lesson. Whatever their reason for not asking, the bottom line is if your students aren't asking questions, they are not learning.

ASK ME A QUESTION!

Go preemptive with your approach to questions. Let students exhaust their questions on a point, topic and/or assignment. Never *ask* them if they have any questions. Rather, state: *ask me a question.*

How you present this imperative statement is also important. If you state it in a commanding tone, you'll probably scare the class. However, if you state it with *positive expectation* in your voice, you'll make further strides.

It's kind of fun because it always catches the students off guard. If they sit there, doing their Easter Island Head impression, say, "C'mon ask me a question. Validate me as a teacher. I have to have questions."

Or, you might say, "Well, ask me a question you already know the answer to."

So, the questions will come. Sometimes, they will be silly. Answer them, regardless, as if they were important. Whenever a student asks a question, effusively praise that question, *not* the questioner. Thank the questioner without sarcasm. Praise the question; thank the questioner.

Sometimes, if the question is painfully obvious, which we sometimes equate with stupid, you might say, "That's a question that someone is thinking! Good!"

Or if it is a super-duper question, you can say, "That is an awesome question because that question concerns why this assignment is significant. Excellent!"

Throw out this "Ask me a question" directive at logical breaks, particularly during a difficult passage of instruction or reading or, in the earlier stages, right before they begin an assignment.

The outcome is that students become conditioned to ask questions. At the beginning, of course, it will be a bit painful and probably awkward, but as the school year wears on, they will become more adept at the skill, moving into their assignments with vigor and understanding. You'll find that you have to say it less and less.

If you need further persuasion, consider this strategy a preemptive disciplinary precaution. Students who *understand* what they are supposed to do are less likely to engage in off-task behavior.

Eventually, the questions will dribble down to silence. Don't let them start their assignment until all questions are asked and answered. Students may lean forward in their seats. The anticipatory moment between the confidence of how to begin an assignment and the directive—"You have x minutes. Go for it!"—is beautiful. No other word to describe it.

Of course, they may have more questions along the way during an assignment. In your role as facilitator, you will walk around the class, responding to those questions. If you get a question that might impact the entire class in some way, hold up your hand, stop the class, and address it.

For example, "Number Three has an error, everyone. It should be ____. Sorry about that!" Then, carry on.

Do you see how the No More Questions scenario would have been so much more effective if the teacher had procedures in place for his off-topic stuff? Moreover, do you see how he might have drawn the students in with the directive to ask him a question?

After a while of doing this, students begin to move away from the goofy questions into those that will truly serve their learning. Additionally, they are not afraid to ask what something means. Only then can they even begin to learn.

SOCRATIC QUESTIONING

Depending on the course, you might want to take time to address *how* to ask questions. How do we know what questions to ask? And, if asking questions is a way students learn, why, then, do students *not* ask questions? Why do they just sit there, nod their heads, and fail?

The Socratic method and Bloom's Taxonomy can go hand in hand, moving from lower-order questioning (knowledge) to higher-order questioning (evaluation). The Socratic method must be taught, however. Students need to know *how* to ask questions. Let's take a look at how the two might work together.

First Level

Clarification (Socrates)
    Why do you say that?

How does ___relate to ___?
What is ___?
Knowledge (Bloom)
  How would you describe ___?
  What is ___?

Second Level

Probing Assumptions (Socrates)
  What could we assume instead?
  How can you verify or disprove that assumption?
Comprehension (Bloom)
  How would you state this in your own words?
  What might be an example of ___?

Third Level

Probing Reason/Evidence (Socrates)
  What is ___similar or analogous to?
  What do you think causes ___to happen?
  Why does ___seem to ___?
Application (Bloom)
  How does ___relate to ___?
Analysis (Bloom)
  How does ___compare/contrast to ___?
  How can we differentiate ___?

Fourth Level

Viewpoints/Perspectives (Socrates)
  What might be an alternative?
  What are the strengths and weaknesses?
Synthesis (Bloom)
  What might you predict/infer from ___?
  What solutions might you suggest for ___?

Fifth Level

Probing Implications and Consequences (Socrates)
  What generalizations could be made?
  What are the consequences of the assumption?

Evaluation (Bloom)
    Do you agree that ___?
    How would you decide about?

Sixth Level

Questioning the Question (Socrates)
    What is the point of the question?
    Why should we ask this question?
Evaluation (Bloom)
    What criteria would you use to assess ___?

It doesn't matter whether you're teaching algebra I or western civilization, the skill of question posing is crucial. The progressive movement and tasks can be successfully aligned if we help students see what they are through questions.

This is the first time I've seen Bloom posed as questions. The taxonomy is always in verb form, so this is very helpful. ~ AnnMarie

To teach how to ask questions, you might begin with a simple object, such as a coffee mug or a doo-dad you happen to have on your desk. Put the object in the middle of the class first, for all to see. Then you might consider having it passed around. The assignment, you should explain, is for students to ask you questions about this object. Give them the answers, eventually, but the goal is for them to come up with an exhaustive list of questions.

The obvious questions will come first: *What is it? How old is it? Where did you get it?*

All of the students should write down the questions asked, leaving some space for the response. You can model for them on the overhead.

Inevitably, the questions will end up somewhere in comprehension or dip into analysis. Application, synthesis, and evaluation will probably be generally lacking. This is your teachable moment: to model these types of questions.

Why are you asking us to ask you questions about a mug? (Evaluation)
Why should we care about a mug? (Evaluation)
How do we know this is your mug? (Evidence/Argument)

After it seems you've exhausted questions, give a couple of responses that might generate more questions. If you use objects that have significance for you, such as a coffee mug a former student, who subsequently won some sort of award, gave you, or a toy that your mother gave you when you broke your arm, the questions will be richer. Have the students record responses as they see fit. Then, explain to them that they have approached this object from all facets of learning (also praise them for their input).

"Now," you might say, "let's take a look at Socrates. Say that with me, 'Socrates.' This guy was the King of Questions."

(A nifty handout of Socratic questions is helpful and relatively easy to make.) "This is your question guide," you can say. "Ask me a question or make an observation about this question guide."

Eventually, they will get the idea that there are *x* number of ways to ask questions. And, by golly, there really isn't a dumb question after all! The students should be permitted to use these handouts as references for as long as they need them. You can surely imagine the impact of a student asking, after reading a particularly difficult choral ode in *Oedipus Tyrannos*, "How does this ode fit in with what we just read, though?"

The *teacher* didn't ask this question.
The *student* did.

When students ask the questions, the class's behavior is more on-task and, thus, attentive to the lesson. Don't miss that point! This strategy is not only to instill critical thinking but also to keep students' attention. In short, students like to hear what other students have to say!

Again, consider our adult class. The presenter is probably great, but when one of your peers has some clever input or a solid question, your attention naturally spikes.

Students will definitely listen to what other students have to say. It can also be a pride or competition thing. "Well, if she's asking a question and making it look as if she knows about this subject, then I can too!" Student A's question often validates Student B's question as well as the desire to ask a question. ~ Christina

For lower-level classes, you might take this strategy one step further, using your overhead list of the class roster, with all of the students' names or even the seating chart. When a student asks a question, put a little dot next to his/her name.

"By the end of the discussion," you can explain, "each of you will need at least three dots to receive your grade for discussion today. That means you've participated at least three times. To get a dot, you can either ask a question or respond to a question."

It might be a little stilted and awkward for the first few times, but after a while a shift will occur because you won't need the dots anymore. The students will ask questions on their own.

You mentioned how important it is to not only get the student to start asking questions, but to teach them to ask the "right" questions. As the teacher is supposed to be the bridge for the students' learning, is it not an agreeable tactic for the teacher to ask the question if it fulfills that function as a bridge?

For instance, you tell the students to ask a question (love that bit), and you get the entire volley thrown at you. However, things aren't quite progressing in the direction you'd hoped. Would it not be prudent to ask a question in their place to guide them on to the proper path? ~ Daniel

The short answer to Daniel's question is "Yes!" It's a sly game we play, presenting questions that will (hopefully) lead students in the direction they should go. Because teachers are the subject-matter experts, we have an idea of where we want the student to go, so it's incumbent upon us to predict the "volley" and prepare the "return" question—all in an effort to get students on the appropriate thinking track.

Eventually, though, the teacher lessens the use of his/her questions. For example, going from say, 95/5 percent (teacher/student) to 90/10, 80/20 to 75/25 and so on . . . until the learning is student driven. The messages this strategy sends are:

My teacher wants me to be involved in this class.
I'm expected to ask questions.
I can ask questions without fear of rancor.
I have the tools to learn for myself.

Absolutely! We're giving the students the words that they don't currently have. They know what they want to know, but they don't know how to say it.

One of the strategies that helped my students was what could loosely be called an FAQ Wall. It had many reminders that began with: "If you want to know this . . . say this . . ." The students did not experience the anxiety about how to ask and, thus, asked more. ~ AnnMarie

ANSWERING QUESTIONS

This is very grey area. We do supply answers, but we ultimately want students to survive on their own. We aren't going to be there at testing time, when they need to know how to cope. Again, this is a scaffolding process that may take some time because it goes against student conditioning or, at least, their perceived conditioning.

Actually, they've learned that whining long enough and loud enough eventually yields results. The water-drip-torture method does that. They just keep whining and whiningandwhiningingandwh—until teachers just break down. Thus, *your* conditioning also needs deconditioning.

After one has the class comfortable with *asking* questions, the goal is to make them comfortable with *answering* them too. How do you help students become comfortable enough to "risk" giving an answer?

Wait time is a solid strategy after a teacher has asked a question, but we tend to get impatient (mostly due to our own pressure to perform as borne down upon us from above). Interestingly though, when students do the asking, wait time isn't so much of an issue.

This strategy is again a form of progressive modeling. Explain to students that on this first assignment, you will show them how to "find" the answers. They're familiar with this strategy, so it should go quickly. For lower-level questions, it will probably be a matter of directing them to a point in the text: "Let's take another look at paragraph two, under Water Cycle, to find the answer."

Then, on a subsequent assignment, step out of answering lower-order questions. They have demonstrated their ability to find a concrete answer in a text, so on the next assignment, they are responsible, as a class, to address that particular level of question.

For higher-order questions, the goal is to move them into analysis, synthesis, and evaluation on the basis of the response to the lower-order questions. "Janey asked how old the narrator is. Let's see if we can figure that out from what the author writes about this character, here." (reread)

As you move through the information, you step further and further back out of the questions. Perhaps the most difficult aspect of literary analysis, or reading in general, is that there may not be a *correct* answer. There is a *best* answer, however. This concept is quite relieving to students as it pertains to state exams and writing, particularly. The best answer contains the best argument, when the question is interpretive or subjective.

Eventually, you'll want to be completely out of class discussions. Make sure you read that correctly: *you're out of the picture* on the topic. The students will *ask* and *answer*. The creation of this atmosphere will largely be due to the introduction to the Socratic method. Their questions cannot be "stupid" because this really smart guy who lived thousands of years ago asked them.

Thus, the preemptive strategy of presenting the arsenal of questions resolves the judgments that sometimes emerge in these discussions. Since the *judgment* of a student's question or answer by another student can shut the discussion down faster than a Bugatti Veyron, the facilitator's role must be explicit. By taking most of the potential for rancor away step-by-step, the class will have a much more in-depth experience with the material.

Staying out of the discussion is somewhat painful, but so necessary. If you're patient, more than likely their thinking will move in the right direction. From this exercise, you'll also realize how quickly you used to jump in and save them.

Don't save them.

When things matter the most, we won't be there to save them. When things matter the most, they are on their own. We tell them this over and over, but we tend to leave them alone only when they're completing a test. They need this solo practice.

Be assured that we also, as a class, evaluated how well we discussed. We determined what went well and what didn't. In some instances, this was a writing assignment, and in others, it was a discussion. Either way, the evaluation of how they were learning was part of the whole.

Teenagers like to argue—this, we know. They love to have their opinions heard, and they love to evaluate.

As a teenager, being able to prove someone wrong or bring them to your ideal of thinking is a daily goal—the more student driven the discussion, the more likely you'll see full participation! ~ Christina

Capitalize on this stage of their development, moving it in an academic direction with expectations for *how* to handle their arguments and opinions. You'll send these messages: "My teacher believes that I am able to reason, think, create, and respond."

And, more importantly: "My teacher believes that I can do this."

TEXTBOOKS AND CRITICAL THINKING

Textbooks are the teacher's mythical best friend. As far as having a whole bunch of information in one spot for ease of use, yes. You cannot argue the economics of them either, especially as they become digitally available. As far as paving the way to critical thinking and transparent teaching, though, the benefits may not be so obvious. For example, how can we get students to ask their own questions, when the textbook already has those questions outlined? How can you use a textbook to help you model learning authentically?

One of the more powerful experiences you can have working with students is the "double-blind" lesson, which works particularly well as an introduction to a reading or study strategy. Whatever the assignment is, you will be approaching it *as a learner*, modeling effective strategies. They've never read the material; neither have you—double-blind. To do that, you have to ditch the teacher's edition. You have to be on the same page as your students, literally. If you can, you may also want to ditch the textbook, opting for the original, unedited, un-textbooked work.

I had always wanted to read Thoreau's essay "On Civil Disobedience," and never had. I chose that work as the double-blind lesson. (We had access to the text as a supplemental booklet, but if it had been in a textbook, the goal would have been to avoid reading any extras.)

Thus, on equal footing, we began. We made it through a few paragraphs, with the students diligently taking notes, highlighting. The students, interestingly, would have kept going, but I stopped and said, "What?? Wait, wait, wait . . . I don't get this [reference to text]. Does he mean___ or___?"

The conversation moved forward after an epiphany or three. These students were *plowing* through the text with the hope that they would eventually understand. Modeling more inquisitive text interaction (I do tend to talk back to books) provided them with a new strategy and a stronger sense of "we" as a class, with the teacher as facilitator. Eventually, they felt much more comfortable stopping for clarification or sharing of a thought. They wouldn't have done that, though, without modeling.

Try at least one double-blind assignment and poll your students on its effectiveness. Watching a teacher learn, or even struggle, provides numerous benefits.

Our school set aside twenty minutes at the start of every day (we were on block) for state-test preparation. All was well and good except that we had to teach whatever specific "problem" or "passage" that was provided. That is, math teachers taught reading; English teachers taught math. Oh, yes!

Out of this frustration, though, came a beautiful teaching moment. Math is not my strong suit. Nonetheless, the problem involved finding the volume of a cube by solving for a bunch of letters like x and y.

The cube, however, didn't look anything like a cube to my nonmathematical brain. It looked like a huge cross or letter T. I couldn't "see" the cube, and while I'm okay with solving for x (and nothing else) or finding the volume of a cube (and nothing else), I was at a loss at how to put all of these skills together.

One student desperately tried to explain the two-dimensional perspective of a three-dimensional shape from his seat, to no avail. Finally, he got so frustrated, he stole the lesson!

I remember those little test prep sessions! I went up and cut out the little box and taped it together, so that way, we could measure the sides. ~ Zach Russakis

That was it. That was what we needed. The class applauded. I applauded. We solved the problem, and we *all* learned that day.

GET HOT, NOT BOTHERED

Now that you've made it into the meat of your course, your students are ready to ask questions, and you're ready to start making the thematic connections you've worked so diligently to create back in your planning. When we do actually move into presentation of information, though, we tend to dwell on the lower-order thinking (LOT) points and questions before higher-order thinking (HOT) questions. What might happen if we presented things backwards? What if we got *HOT*, first?

Lower-order concerns (e.g., definitions, dates, theories, biographies, and grammar) can be more meaningful when we work "backwards" in the taxonomy, from evaluation and synthesis as the objectives *for* accessing understanding and knowledge. Our students' world is one of LOT information *at a keystroke*, and when compelling them to think towards a higher-order purpose (analysis/evaluation), we provide them with a stronger *desire* to know, comprehend, and apply.

What the student showed us with that cube was HOT, which compelled and drove us to find the answer. Had we just fumbled about with the formulas, we wouldn't have had that powerful moment.

Objectives for lessons can be phrased and presented as higher-order questions, which provide the reason for studying/analyzing whatever "it" is. For example, your objective might be: *The student will compare and contrast two authors, one from the nineteenth century and one from the twenty-first century.*

From that objective, you want your students to arrive at this question: *Why is the analysis of authors from these two specific time periods relevant and/ or significant?*

Then, the idea is to get the student to arrive at his or her answer in *movement*: what they think, based on the information known and gathered *before*, *during*, and *after* the lesson. The answer *shifts* and moves as the LOT is collected, but the motivation is HOT.

Particularly in those required core academic courses, using student-driven HOT questions is a key to bringing out a willingness to learn. Although at first, you may have to convey the significance of the lesson/unit/term/year, eventually, the students must fly solo.

We need thinkers in the classroom, but we are not harvesting this generation's capacity for thinking. Compelling them to think for a HOT purpose (synthesis/evaluation) helps provide them with a reason to bother accessing the LOT details.

I didn't go into teaching high school because I loved teenagers. I went into teaching because I enjoyed my field, and I wanted to share my knowledge. However, that reasoning can lead us astray in our pursuit of ideal class experiences. Sharing knowledge is only the smallest part. It is the LOT of teaching.

The most pivotal classroom memory I have didn't happen in a classroom at all.
As Floridians, we dealt with our share of hurricanes. However, in 2004, with

both Frances and Jeanne leaving a path of destruction in their wake, it put a completely new perspective on what was essential to life. Streets and homes were flooded. The school wasn't accessible due to the extent of the water damage. And so, for a while, the twenty-first century lifestyle halted.

It was the beginning of my senior year with AP Lit, and we were set up to read Milton's Paradise Lost. *I know that a group of high schoolers would typically be reveling in not having school for a month.*

But we read.

Some by candlelight, others by flashlight, or those who were fortunate enough to have generators, by the lights from their bedrooms. Keller collected us all in her home, without electricity, to begin discussing the book.

Only a teacher as passionate towards her craft and students would bring them into her home to discuss Milton. ~ Crystal

So, perhaps effective teaching or transparent teaching or HOT teaching isn't teaching at all, but just loving the act of learning.

Chapter Thirteen

Creating and Using
Teacher Evaluations

*Teachers can learn a lot about their students from an eval. It's an excellent op-
portunity to learn how their students think because when students are asked to
criticize their teacher, that's something they'll definitely be interested in enough
to put some thought into. ~ Daniel*

Secondary schools are beginning to use student-based evaluations a bit more,
but these are generally for research or large, grand purposes. However, with
flexible and consistent use, student evaluations can move an entire class experience forward.

One of the components of every assignment or project completed should
include an evaluation. Whether the last question on a test or an end-of-year
evaluation, this feedback is invaluable and truly helps us grow as educators.

Your courses will greatly benefit because the students share what did *and*
didn't work to improve their understanding of the material. For example, the
mini-lectures, which I always prefaced with "This is the boring part!" were
inevitably dubbed "keepers" by the students in their evals of the same. They
found them informative and helpful! Likewise, some of the assignments that
teachers may enjoy, the students find lacking in substance. As high schoolers,
they do possess the ability to suggest alternatives, and we need to tap into
that ability.

*I remember a constant flow of opinion; you were always asking us what we
thought, using that information to determine whether we'd learned. It was the
learning process of the class. ~ AnnMarie*

In addition to specific lesson evaluations, encourage them to evaluate you
in your role as an educator. After all, they are your target audience, and it

stands to reason that their opinions on how things work matter. Just as you give students mid-term and semester grades, the students can grade you.

One colleague, who liked the face value of this idea, tried to use it. He got angry with the results, though. "They don't like anything!" he said, "Nothing is going to be good enough for them!"

However, he put forward his evaluation without building rapport and without establishing an understanding of what learning/teaching was. You can't just lob an evaluation out there; you have to build up to it. Without a foundation of rapport and trust, it will fall short of being beneficial.

His students rebelled, taking the opportunity to provide some extremely harsh criticism. Underlying this criticism, though, was the core of the problem: you can't ask for something and then fall apart. This is why you'd need to establish the environment for evaluation beforehand—when students have nothing to rebel against!

EN ROUTE EVALS

You have many options for obtaining feedback en route: written responses, quick discussions, class surveys, or even sticky notes. En route evals can be anonymous, but most students are usually quite open to assessing an assignment, lesson, or unit. You can always consider including an evaluation as part of the unit/chapter test too.

The first time you have students assess an assignment or lesson, you'll want to be very explicit and clear about it. For example:

> Okay, guys! Today, I'm going to need your input! Last year's students asked me to change this lesson to make it more interesting, so while we work on it, I want you to think about whether it works for you. At the end of this lesson, we'll talk more about it. Ask me a question before we get started.

Of course, if the lesson is completely new to the course, you'll need to say so, or if you've never taught the course before, say so. Additionally, if the lesson is a keeper from the previous year, identify it as such with the disclaimer that the current class could enhance it. Generally, this evaluation concept will be new to the students, so they'll have questions. After a while, it will become a regular part of the everyday ideal class experience.

TEACHING THE CONCEPT OF EVALUATION

Because this approach will be new to students, you'll have to move them up to your expectations. Sometimes, they'll be afraid to hurt your feelings, which is quite sweet, but not conducive to improving the class experience. Here is an example of the spectrum of responses you might receive on a first eval of a lesson:

This lesson was good. I liked it!

or

This really sucked.

Here's where you must make an important distinction. *You* are not your lessons. *You* are not good or bad. *You* are not your course.

Do you get that?

You can neither jump for joy nor melt into a puddle of self-pity at these general comments. You must get at the meat of these generalizations. What, specifically, made the lesson good? Why did they like this or that? What parts of the lesson should be kept or thrown out? Why, specifically, did it suck?

One common criticism you'll get at first is, "This is stupid." Pay attention to this one because it really means, "I don't understand or see the connection of this to me."

While our first impulse may be to wish the student to a penal colony on Mars for calling Shakespeare, Angelou, Newton, Cisneros, or Ayn Rand *stupid*, do resist. You'll need to be prepared to allow the other students in the class to explore the connection—your thoughts on connection didn't permeate.

Those students who have seen a connection will, if you've created a warm, receptive environment, feel comfortable enough to explain the connection they see. By doing so, you'll allow your "This is stupid" critic to make an even stronger connection.

This level of evaluative analysis, for those keeping track, is an example of critical thinking too. For lower-level students, you will move them up a notch by the notion of the concept (once again). Upper-level students will be challenged to go more in-depth with their thinking. The merits of evaluation are twofold: gaining feedback on your course and enhancing the students' ability to think analytically, to reason critically, and to evaluate, well, *somewhat* tactfully.

KEEPING EVALS FRESH

As you use evaluations, you'll want to make sure they don't become stale. The students will become complacent and so will you. Thus, you'll want to change up your approach as much as possible. Make it homework one time. Make it a quick discussion. Have students evaluate in their own discussion as if you were not present.

The latter idea is quite challenging but rewarding. In one of my creative writing courses at college, student writers sat in the "hot seat." We submitted copies of our work to the whole class, and on our day of criticism, we were not allowed to speak. We had to listen and take notes. Our peers talked about our submissions as though we were not present at all. Uncomfortable? You bet!

However, the experience is eye-opening for both the recipients and the critics. The critics learned how to express themselves more effectively, and the recipient learned how to listen—both valuable skills that translate effectively to the classroom.

You have an opportunity to make this evaluation experience a significant learning gain for both you and your students. Be creative and innovative to keep the evaluations alive and breathing.

MID-TERM EVAL

For their opening assignment on the day of your mid-term grade, the students should either find a form on the board to copy and complete or an actual mid-term form. It can be very basic (see figure 13.1).

Students can indicate their general opinions by circling the appropriate criticism. If you score less than average significantly, address it in class. Find out what they're thinking.

As the assignment is anonymous, you'll find it a very handy way to ensure that you are meeting their expectations. If your students need greater incentive, consider giving a grade (twenty-five points) based on handing in the assignment without actually looking at it until later. This is easily accomplished by writing the student's name down as he/she submits a folded piece of paper.

NINE WEEKS' GRADES

Asking students to write a paragraph works best for this level of evaluation, but of course, you could create a form just as easily. Remind them that you *want* criticism! The desire for criticism also serves to defuse some students who would otherwise act out. For some reason, a teacher who is self-critical and open to criticism just doesn't catch as much flack from students. However, they have to justify your grade with reasoning, just as you justify their grades with scores and comments.

Let them use any of their notes or previous evaluations to help them out. Because this is an open assignment, allowing them to discuss with their classmates might also prove fruitful. This approach will entail students get-

```
          Ms. K's Mid-Term Progress Report


  Instructions: Circle one evaluation for each category.


                    Attendance


    Excellent      Average   Needs Improvement   Poor


                 Assignment returns


  Excellent     Average     Needs Improvement       Poor


                     Behavior


  Excellent     Average   Needs Improvement   Poor
```

Figure 13.1.   Sample Teacher Mid-Term Progress Report

ting up, walking to another seat, and talking to a friend, so prepare yourself for unquiet.

Students will take this seriously if you take it seriously. If you really want their input, you will get valuable material. Explain that you want to be the best you can be for the sake of the class. These actions support the message: "My teacher cares about how she teaches."

I vaguely recall that we did evaluations. Although, in this case, that's a good thing. Those times when I was asked my opinion on a lesson (that I actually remember) are those that stirred up resentment because afterwards I felt that either I'd been ignored or that my opinion didn't matter. The whole thing was merely a purposeless exercise.

There's little I hate more than when someone, especially a teacher, stirs up my passion only to then demonstrate its irrelevance in the actual scheme of things. The fact that I don't specifically recall your evals with any of that bitterness means that you considered and cared about the opinions. It wasn't a wasted effort. ~ Daniel

FINAL EVALUATION

The final evaluation can be far more elaborate. You may even want to create it earlier in the year. Copy one for each student, keeping a master document on file. The form is roughly broken down into categories of classroom management, student rapport, course expectations, and strengths/weaknesses. Through a series of prompts, the student should evaluate the course and the teacher. Some questions to consider might be:

> Has this course met your expectations? Why or why not?
> What can I do to improve as a teacher?
> What can I do to improve this course for next year's students?

From these forms, on the last days of school, the class can discuss any weaknesses in the course or teaching style. These evaluations will help your courses become increasingly successful. Students will be quite open about which assignments/units/projects worked well and which did not. Figure 13.2 shows a sample layout of this form.

> *I thoroughly enjoyed end-of-the year evaluations. Also, if it wasn't school-man-*
> *dated, it meant that the teacher cared what the students thought and was taking*
> *the first step to becoming a better educator. That was important to us. ~ Christina*

For example, in my first year of teaching Drama I, the students were required to do a final project on some aspect of theatre. This, they claimed, was quite boring, so why didn't I do a play with my Drama I class? We bandied the idea about and determined that, yes, this could be done. And the Drama One Showcase of One-Acts was born.

> *As a member of one of your first drama classes, I remember that final project! I felt*
> *very privileged and honored to be asked what I thought. The projects were okay,*
> *but very boring to complete. On paper, they must have looked fantastic, though, be-*
> *cause they included so many standards. I'm so glad your later students understood*
> *that my class had a say in the change of curriculum! ~ AnnMarie*

Year two students were told that, based on the previous classes' input, this was what we were going to do. Consider for a moment the impact of hearing that your peers have made this suggestion from the teenagers' perspective, where friends hold more credibility than adults. Also, consider the message received: "My teacher cares about what I think."

After the first end-of-year showcase, I again presented students with the evaluations. "Did this work? Was it too hard? Did you find it a relevant learning experience at this level of drama?" I asked.

English Two End-of-Year Evaluation

This is an anonymous evaluation of the course, the class, and the teacher. Please, don't write your name on it! Be as honest as you can, and remember, what you write will help next year's students!

The Course:

What do you think about the course, now that you've completed it? Did it meet your expectations? Was it too difficult, too easy? What can be done to improve it?

*****

The Class:

Describe your class experience. How did you feel when you came to class every day? Did you look forward to it, or did you dread it? Why? What can be done to improve it?

*****

The Teacher:

What can I do to improve my teaching methods? Was there anything that you felt was out-of-place or needed to be done more often? Why? Overall, what kind of teacher did I project to you?

*****

Assignments:

Please note at least one assignment that you really liked as a "keeper" assignment. Also, let me know if there are any assignments that need to be changed or eliminated and why.

Figure 13.2.   Sample End-of-Year Evaluation Form

My concern was that doing a play would be a bit too difficult for this level of student. However, steadfast input from that group assured me that this was the highlight of their year. Many expressed a sense of pride in themselves and their class. Pride in their work. (And believe me, they worked hard on these short plays! It took patience, perseverance, and creativity.) Moreover, their parents were thrilled to see them perform.

Without my evaluation forms, I may never have moved in this direction. I would have thought it was too much for them to handle. Boy, they proved me wrong! The input of students on both the course and my teaching methods kept me on the path to reaching them in ways that they understood and truly cared about.

Ironically, most of the changes invoked on these forms generally involved higher expectations. What? Students recommending more work, and potentially more difficult work? What's that?

A willingness to learn.

THOSE WHO OPPOSE

There are those, in much higher educational realms than I, who find that students are incapable of any sort of valid evaluation. However, that's why the need for *teaching* evaluation is so crucial. Generally speaking, the lower the level of students, the more they need to understand this level of thought. Thus, it is our goal to move them "up" in their thinking. How can we do that if we do not give them the opportunity? How can we do that if we just say, "Nope, they can't handle it. Forget it!'"?

Teach them how to handle it. Teach them how to measure in other ways than just present satisfaction. Teach them higher criteria than their current set of expectations. Many times, I would find myself frustrated because students' expectations of me were too *low*.

"C'mon, guys!" I would say, "Did you really like this part of this lesson? Wasn't it a bit awkward? Let's be real here. This could be better; don't lower your expectations of me or this class for one minute!"

You always "kept it real" in our classes—that was one of the main things we all appreciated about you. Your expectations of us stayed high, and you wanted our expectations of you to be high as well. ~ Christina

This particular component of teaching can be difficult to digest. However, your students are your most *natural* critics. They see you every day and know you better than your administrators or even your fellow teachers. Their opinions and critiques matter.

Their understanding of the "everyday" you is valuable. While anyone can certainly evaluate a teacher on a single lesson or in a drive-by observation, they just won't have the whole picture. Students will. Through mutual trust in this facet of the class, you'll become a better educator, and your students will enhance their critical-thinking skills. Plus, you'll need that trust as you also begin dishing out the grades.

Chapter Fourteen

We Are Such Stuff as Grades Are Made On

I have found that many students aren't really excited about learning, but they are excited about getting decent grades so that they can get into a decent college. Those grades are so important to them that they will do almost anything to get them . . . with the possible exception of actually studying.

I have rarely seen a population work so hard to avoid learning things. Not much willingness to learn, nor has there ever been. ~ *Veteran teacher*

Who are grades for, anyway? Are they for the students or the teachers? What do they actually mean?

Assessing, evaluating, and giving an arbitrary number or letter to ascribe a tangible level of quality for what constitutes a subjective "something" is necessary but sometimes arduous. While there are definitely right and wrong answers in history, math, and laws of science, there is such an ambiguity to the response of a person to an event or story or character or an argumentative assertion.

Students, ostensibly, *work* for a grade, and disrupting that thinking is refreshing. When the focus is on the grade and not the learning process, there is a forced abruptness, a full stop. The message implied is, "You're finished. Move on."

This isn't what we want, is it? Don't we want students to understand how learning builds upon itself? It's so much easier to grade the lower-order stuff though! Quick and dirty. Grading or assessing higher-order stuff takes more time. However, the teacher's focus on the *process* of learning leads students down a more in-depth, valuable path.

Like it or not, our philosophy of grades and grading make a huge difference to the class experience.

Keller was a teacher who cared if the students were "getting it." She wasn't going to hand out a passing grade for a half-assed attempt at assignments. I

know there were students who were completely intimidated by the fact that she
was invested in the student, not a test. ~ Crystal

This investment that Crystal remembers was produced by grading to objectives. If *learning* or *application* is the objective, then the approach to grading should follow. If *performance* or *correctness* is the goal, then the grading should support that end. It's when we get these two objectives jumbled up that we run into trouble, students falter, and we fall behind under that mountain of paperwork.

As a student, it's important that I know where I stand in the class. It gives me a
sense of how the teacher grades, and I can use that as a tool to adapt to that class.
It also opens the door for me to ask the teacher how I can do something better.
I remember in your class that you were always so prompt about giving us our
grades back or feedback on the spot. I always felt that I knew where I stood grade-
wise in your class. Also, I can't tell you how many experiences I have had where
I would get a paper back, and I could tell it was just busy work. The teacher gave
it a check mark and barely looked at it. Those types of teachers made me not even
want to try. Why waste my time when the teacher doesn't care? ~ Tori

TURNAROUND TIME:
MEETING THE CLASS'S EXPECTATION

Tori brings up the bane of all teachers' existence. It never fails. You get a batch of essays or tests or projects or whatever, and you just don't get to it. Then, another batch flies in, attaching itself to the first batch, creating a *clump*. The clumps then grow exponentially of their own accord; until finally, you're surrounded by what teacherologists refer to as a *convergence*: i.e., papers held together with rubber bands and/or paper clips, skillfully and obsessively sorted using an alternating-perpendicular method.

There goes your weekend.

You pack everything up into tote bags or other nonesuch, already peeved before you've even begun. Consider how that attitude may or may not impact your approach to grading. If we go into grading with this heavy despair, it will never be used as it should be: as an indication of where the student *is* in his/her learning experience.

GRADE SMARTER

A paperwork convergence can be less daunting if you make and keep a commitment of a turnaround time. I told my students that, for the most part, their work would be returned, graded, the next day. In some instances, I might take two days, but my personal goal was a single-day turnaround.

Before you launch into the huffing and puffing of how this simply cannot be done, first consider the impact on the students.

Whoa. My teacher returns my work the next day?

It makes an impression. Further, it's motivational for both of us. Moreover, it is pedagogically sound. For example, let's say you have a lesson on creating simple sentences, followed by a lesson on run-on structures—a somewhat logical progression, if the students get what a simple sentence is.

If you don't grade their assignments for three days, *how do you know* whether or not you can even move on to the next step?

One colleague put it this way, "I don't get it. In the business world, I was on top of my game with organization. I was the best at what I did, always knew where everything was, and always got everything done ahead of time. What's my problem with grading? Why do I get so far behind?"

One possibility is that the teacher's instructional (in-class) time is so overwhelming and stressful that any subsequent planning/grading time (out of class) is used to *decompress*. He or she simply has no *energy* to grade for this type of turnaround time.

Another possibility is that teachers just keep plugging along, with a backlog of grading they've ostensibly saved for the weekend, and the entire purpose for grades is lost. Papers are returned superficially—behold the check mark! Students don't use them for future reference (as we might like) because we're already past that point in the unit. Thus, the assignments are shoved in the backpack without as much as a blink. Useless.

I loved the teachers who returned our assignments quickly—it gave me much-needed motivation. I wanted to do my best. So, when a teacher returned my grade quickly, I was able to assess where I stood with the expectations I had of myself. ~ Christina

The motivation Christina refers to clearly connects to the pedagogy of quick turnaround time. Consider what happens when you grade the assignment before the next class. More than likely, you have taken the time to create a unit in which the lessons build on each other, and you return the assignment the next day.

You have all the data right in front of you as to how you should proceed. If the students "got" it, then you have a solid reference for them to use on this next lesson. They will "see" the connections between the assignments. If they didn't "get" the previous lesson, then you can redirect them and move them forward, based on the misunderstanding.

"All well and good," say the naysayers, "in theory. However, it is impossible to keep up with the multitude of work I assign and what the district requires. Also, the students won't work unless we give them grades for every last little thing."

Your district does have requirements for work, but those requirements don't necessarily correspond to a huge number of *assignments*. (There are always exceptions, but hear me out anyway.) They generally refer to a number of *grades*. I was always surprised that by the time the nine weeks ended, I'd far exceeded the required number of grades, even with my turnaround policy, because the assignments were stacked. AnnMarie had a similar experience:

> *My field experience was a mandated eight grades a week, which led to over-looked content and frustrated students. It was a flat-line of grades; nothing really seemed to matter. The number of grades certainly didn't translate into learning; they only served to stress everyone out.*
>
> *However, I did find a way, by stretching the very constraints that held us in. One assignment could count for two or more grades if it was both completed and presented.* ~ *AnnMarie*

If your district is operating on a system that mandates what assignments are to be completed on what day in what week, see if you can find a way to tweak it. Not for your sake, but towards student mastery. Students who fully and completely understand a few things *well* are better off than those who have superficially gone over a lot of things. (Do we want to go a mile *deep* or a mile *long*?)

ASSESSING THE MEANS AND THE END: CATEGORICAL WEIGHTS OF DOING AND DONE

The first thing to do is to create solid categorical weights. Roughly, we can divide grades up into: (1) what the students do *in* the class with the teacher; (2) what the students do *outside* of the class on their own; (3) *presentation* of work; and (4) formal *assessments*:

In-Class Assignments
Homework/Quizzes
Area of Discipline Category (Essays, Lab Notebook, etc.)
Tests/Projects

Where you place the greatest categorical weight, if your system allows, can make all the difference. One school of thought says, "Make them equal. Twenty-five percent per category."

However, giving the *doing* categories (in-class work) greater weight and the *done* category (tests/projects) less weight will provide you with a better indication of whether you're grading effectively and whether the student is actually learning.

For example, if the student completes all of her daily work (which will be the majority of assignments) and has a C, but her test grades are Fs, you may have an issue with your approach, no matter what your weights are. Something is amiss. The student may fail, and she shouldn't.

Double-check your approach to those daily assignments. Are you giving check marks or points for simply submitting the assignment, or are you ascertaining *how well* the student approached that work?

Likewise, if the student has Fs on all of her daily work, but gets As on her tests, then again, something is amiss. Potentially, the student is cheating, or maybe you are using multiple-choice tests, which are readily passed with good test-taking strategies. That student will likely pass the nine weeks unless you've weighted your categories appropriately. Should she pass your class? Why or why not?

I used to get a big kick out of student reactions to my grading system, which heavily weighted work done in class. Whether it was active discourse in AP Language or rehearsals in Drama III, the priority was clear: how you're *doing* stuff is more important than that final grade (the *done*).

Consider these weights:

In-Class Assignments 50 percent
Homework/Quizzes 10 percent
Tests/Projects 10 percent
Area-of-Discipline Category (Essays, Lab Notebook, etc.) 30 percent

Here's where it gets tricky! If you have thirty in-class assignments, for example, the *percentage* of the thirty assignments that the student completed will be his grade in that category.

For example, if Sean turns in fifteen out of the thirty assignments, all perfect/satisfactory scores, his *average* in-class assignment grade will be 50 percent. That grade is half of his entire grade for the nine weeks. Figure 14.1 shows you how weighting can more accurately reflect where the student stands.

Sean's not doing well on his daily in-class work, where the bulk of learning occurs. His grades, when weighted, indicate that something's going on in class. Additionally, if the student is squeaking by on tests with a D, the instruments may not be valid, and they're worth a closer look. What does seem to be working well for Sean is the lab work. Identifying what's going on in labs that's different, better, or poorly assessed will give you a much sharper view of the whole.

# Grades in Categories	Average of category
30 In-Class	50%
10 Homework	67%
3 Tests	62%
5 Labs	70%

Student Grade with Weights:
58

Student Grade without Weights:
62

Figure 14.1. Weighted Grade versus Unweighted Grade

The goal is not to punish the student by using a system that gives him a lower grade. Rather, it is to emphasize the need for the student to participate in the bulk of his learning experience. It would only have to happen once, in the first nine weeks, for the student to realize that he *must* do the in-class work to be successful. What will occur as a result (if your in-class work is on track) is he will make *leaps* in learning gains, not just steps.

If the goal is for students to learn, and most learning takes place in the class, then the grade for that component of the class will, and should, accurately reflect where the student's comprehension is. You will have a better idea of whether this student is learning or not, and from there, you and the student can more effectively determine a plan of action, if necessary.

SCAFFOLDING AND GRADING

Do you think grading should differ for each class? For example, in intensive reading should credit be given for the student trying? I wonder because some students in intensive reading will never understand main idea or author's purpose, but if they are trying to learn, should credit be given? Same with homework: if you do it, you get full credit. If you don't do it, receive a zero? ~ Stacey

Stacey's question is absolutely valid, and certainly lower-level learners need a different approach to their grading and assessment. One tactic that works well with remedial learners is using a grading scaffold: a spectrum that moves from credit for *completion* to credit for appropriate *application* to credit for *correctness* and mastery.

Ground-Floor Grade

Let's say you're working with students on the reading portion of their state test. You'd first give a diagnostic—that is, students complete a passage and questions without any instruction. They receive fifty points simply for *completing* the assignment; however, they will take note of how many responses they get correct/incorrect (their invisible grade). Yes, you'll get a few apathetic submissions, probably with all incorrect responses, but it will prove interesting to them a bit later. Everybody starts off with a good grade and a reward for doing work.

First-Level Grade

Teach students a single *skill*, such as strategy for reading a paragraph: e.g., context clues, question prediction, or selective underlining. Hand them a paragraph (without the questions). Tell them they'll be graded on whether or not they've *done* the strategy.

Teach them a second strategy, using the same paragraph, third, and so on. Until finally, they read a paragraph and every strategy is represented. Each time, you provide a grade for *completion*. If the student does not complete every strategy as you've taught, hand the assignment back to them for *completion*.

Second-Level Grade

Tell students they're going to be graded on *how well* they apply all the strategies to a new paragraph. This is the first true evaluation. Be clear in your expectations: you're looking for substitutions for difficult words written on the side, important underlining and clear predictions (and any other strategies you might have presented).

You won't be giving them the questions to the passage just yet, only the reading. Most students will perform the strategies well because they won't have the anxiety of the questions.

Third-Level Grade

After you've taught the strategies for reading the passage, now teach the strategies for answering the questions. For example, the 50/50 strategy (marking off the two or three non-answers and choosing between the two remaining) will reinforce the need for students to use the strategy for "best" answer selection. Do not grade the students on correctness; grade them solely on their *application* of the strategy.

Fourth-Level Grade

After a few rounds of learning the strategies, the students are now ready for their first *correctness* grade. Again, moving in stages will boost their confidence. If they get the correct answer as a possibility in their 50/50 (even if they haven't actually selected it as the response), they get credit for the response. Again, emphasizing that the approach to the test can be learned.

Fifth-Level Grade

The final level of grading, full performance, should only be presented after every strategy has been mastered. At this point, the student will receive a grade on the number of *correct* answers. Have the student compare the responses between this assignment and the diagnostic side by side.

This scaffolding is not a new idea at all, but it's concrete, which is what lower-level learners need: small victories and steps that work towards the larger goal.

GRADING TO THE OBJECTIVE OF THE ASSIGNMENT

A large majority of my students don't even want their papers back. They tell me just to recycle them. I feel like I waste my time going through them, correcting the grammar or making comments here and there. My thinking was always that I could make connections with my students on their work, but then, they don't even look at it. ~ Stacey

This is an issue that pervades all subjects and wears teachers down—the redoing of the student work! Math teachers diligently work through a student's assignment to show him every step in that proof; English teachers correct every mechanical error. By the time we're done, we're exhausted!

Grading to the objective means that you only grade for the goal of that assignment—not every aspect of the submission. Daily, in-class assignments are, by nature, relatively short, and/or they have a definitive single purpose. For example, you're not teaching the entire history of the Civil War in one day. You might be teaching what happened at Ft. Sumter. Your assignment is structured to determine whether or not the student understands what happened at Ft. Sumter. With that objective in mind, your grade should be pretty quick. Ask yourself: *did the student get it or not?*

He either got it, "sorta" got it, or didn't get it at all. You have eighty assignments to grade. You offer fifty points for it, keeping in mind that thirty points equates to a degree of *sorta*. How long should this assignment take you to grade, given your knowledge of the material? If you've got a clear objective for the assignment and you stay away from any stray issues, it will probably take you less than twenty minutes to mark the work and five minutes to input it.

If you find that less than three-quarters of your class got it, then you'll need to reconsider your approach to that lesson on Ft. Sumter. This is what grading is supposed to do for teachers—help us see where the students are *after* we've taught.

If you really want to delve into writing mechanics, consider doing so only after you've graded to your objective. If you see a class-wide pattern of error (topical or mechanical), you'll want to address it as a follow-up or revision assignment, if merited.

To identify a pattern, scan one or two submissions of students who represent lower- and middle-level work. What seems to be consistently in error? What do you see as a pattern? By addressing it to the entire class, you won't find yourself writing the same thing over and over. How tiring is that? Plus, the students do the *work*. The student will naturally use the graded assignment as the basis for the revision, warranting its use.

GRADING LARGER ASSIGNMENTS

For those assignments that are lengthier and have a bit more bulk and purpose, you'll want to stagger them. For example, if you have five classes of American history, why make all of the history projects due on the same day? Why not stagger the due dates, if possible?

I'm not sure why the need to have every class on the same page has pervaded the classroom. (Perhaps administrators/school districts have an answer to this one?) Are we truly expecting every class to function in the same manner? How ironic. The push for individualized learning with compartmentalized thinking doesn't work. The two ideologies are at paradoxical odds.

The perception that if you have three classes of course X, each class should be engaging, learning, and submitting assignments on the same day, is inherently flawed. This approach does *not* ease your stress. Yes, on the surface it seems logical, but just for kicks, try a different approach. Is it easier to grade thirty projects or a hundred? Which paper clump seems less daunting?

If you must create a huge influx of work for yourself, make sure that students are submitting them on logical days for *you*, not them. The worst due date for an assignment is a Monday. You don't need to "give" the students the weekend. You will have given them ample time to complete their project. Why do this to yourself?

The best due date for large assignments is the day before a teacher workday or perhaps, a half day. This is another reason why laying out a course outline is helpful! You can pick and choose the "big" dates to your advantage and, ultimately, the students' advantage.

GRADING TRANSPARENTLY

The more students know about where their grades are headed, the better. It's easier to stay on the correct path when we can actually see it. ~ Daniel

One of the most successful ventures schools have undertaken has been the inclusion of online grades and grading programs. Parents and students have the ability to see inside the teacher's grade book, and that effort, as long as the teacher follows through, is very worthwhile.

For those veteran teachers who may be shying away from transparency in grading, consider your past experiences. Are students sometimes belligerent about their grades? Had they known their grades, week by week, how might that knowledge have impacted their attitudes? What have you experienced with students or parents who seemed "shocked" by final grades? Enter the—

Weekly Grade Update

Even though the grades are online, some parents and students don't have a computer or simply don't remember to check.

To ensure that all students are aware of grades at any given moment, consider the use of weekly grade updates. Once a week, present students with a printout of grades, using identification numbers for anonymity.

This weekly report is passed around by the students, providing them with an opportunity to signal the teacher that they want an individual update. Students can highlight or simply circle their ID number to indicate they want a more detailed report. Additionally, this report is kept in the "class folder" of each period's box, so absent students can easily retrieve it. This simple action, which takes all of a moment to print out, has the potential to catch issues before they begin.

More than likely, your district's online program has an option to print a class's grades using the student ID numbers (not names) or another numerical system. If not, consider creating an Excel spreadsheet or even a quick fill-in-the-blank sort of document.

It's a great idea! My district uses a program that we can print out with ID numbers. Also, our district-wide data is all held in one program, and we can export whatever info we need into an Excel spreadsheet. ~ Stacey

Keeping Parents Informed

Remember at the beginning of the year when you got all of those parent e-mails? You made a promise to those parents that you would keep them informed about their children. Your goal, throughout the year, is to keep that promise, and e-mails are the simplest, most direct way to accomplish this goal.

Many schools now have web access for parents to retrieve their child's grades, but many do not know how to do this. Additionally, some may just appreciate a reminder. Thus, your weekly update e-mail will serve a dual purpose: touching base with your parents and keeping them on track with their children.

Weekly updates don't have to be Pulitzer material. They should, however, be upbeat, positive, and include an action for parents to take. Here's an example:

Hello everyone!

Wow! This has been quite a week. We reviewed two different inaugural addresses: President Kennedy's and our current president's. Plus, we took the Oath of Office! Overall, we determined that language has definitely changed since the 1960's, and we're still undecided as to whether that's a good thing or a bad thing.

Ask your child what he or she thinks about the two speeches. Hopefully, they'll remember the famous stuff!

As always, don't forget to check your child's grades at: link at ourschool. com. [PROVIDE LINK] If you have any questions or concerns, please don't hesitate to e-mail me! That's what I'm here for!

Have a great weekend,

[Teacher]

P.S. Would anyone be available on the 23rd to stop in and help us videotape our presentations? Please let me know!

This e-mail takes about two minutes to write and send BCC to a group designated as "Parents of [course number/grade]." It speaks volumes to parents, and when the time comes that you need a volunteer or want them to come to the school for some reason, you can imagine the response: *positive all round.*

Also, consider the ramifications of attending a parent conference, when the parent greets you with *familiarity*, then turns to the counselor, and says, "Oh, I know just how Shelly's doing in Biology. We're all set. I just need to see . . . "

(Don't forget to smile on your way out.)

The best time to send your updates out is on Thursdays so that parents have the opportunity to catch you before the weekend via e-mail. Then, if necessary, you can follow up with a phone call. More often than not, if there's a question, it will revolve around a discrepancy of whether a student has or has not submitted an assignment.

You and the parent might also begin an e-mail dialogue on the student's needs, which you can then forward to the student's counselor. The goal is to meet the students' needs, and maintaining parental contact is crucial to that goal.

HOW YOU GRADE MAKES A DIFFERENCE

I'm sure you've considered the color of your grading already. However, for those who may still be in "red" mode—stop. You may not have gotten the memo, but there is (or at least, should be) a moratorium on red ink. The impact is one of a bleeding paper or at the very least, an angry assessor. You do have a vast spectrum of colors at your disposal: green, purple, pink, turquoise. It's a quick enhancement and worthwhile.

I use purple! Red is just so "in your face." ~ Stacey

I recently read an article that tried to debunk the psychological effect that red marking has on students. I completely disagree. Receiving a paper back from a teacher that is bleeding red ink is disheartening. ~ AnnMarie

How funny! I thought it was just me! I used a green or purple to grade, and I made sure it was a nice pen to write with. ~ Tori

Tori brings up the lesser-known consideration of the quality of the writing instrument. Have you experienced the phenomenon of changing penmanship? For example, if you use pen *A*, you seem to write differently than if you use pen *B*? Try out two different types of pens and see the impact on your penmanship. When we have a nice pen in our hands, we tend to write more legibly.

As teachers, we do love those bargain-brand inexpensive ballpoint pens, don't we? Of course, we do because we have to buy our own supplies for the most part. However, the impression they leave is equally cheap. We write hastily and messily. Additionally, because we are not attached to those pens, they tend to wander off or get lost (as pens are wont to do).

However, that one pen we love? We will hang onto it for dear life. We will hold that pen with care and precision, which reflects in our penmanship and choice of phrase. With the idea that every single little thing we do is sending a message, what message does the simple choice of pen convey?

Are you going to "lose" some pens throughout the school year? Probably. However, if by doing such a small thing, we create a more positive experience for a student, then we have done well. Those things that *are* in our control, let's make sure we take control of them.

THOSE CRAZY HALF DAYS:
WHAT KETCHUP CAN DO FOR YOU!

Half days are both blessing and curse. They're mercifully short, but pedagogically strained. Students justify staying home, telling their parents, "Well, we don't *do* anything."

The end result is usually the loss of a day, despite all efforts. However, if you use that day to your advantage, you may find that students see the benefit in a catch-up or "ketchup" day.

One-on-Ones

Advise students that on Ketchup Days, you'll be calling them in, one at a time, to review their grades. If they need printouts or clarification, you'll provide them. In the meantime, they are to review the list of assignments (on the board or overhead) and double check that they *have* that assignment in their folder. If not, they should be looking for it or completing it.

You might even consider having them put their work in backwards chronological order, for the sake of organization. Whatever works!

As you call each student in, show him/her the grade and any assignments that can be made up. He/she should complete that assignment today— Ketchup Day. Move quickly. The goal is to make sure every student knows what he or she needs to do to improve the grade.

Some Thoughts on What *Not* to Do

It's very disadvantageous to have a test on a half day. Although some teachers claim it's one way to get students to class (is it?), the effort negates itself in the instrument. What kind of test can you give in twenty-five minutes (if you're on traditional scheduling)? If at all possible, avoid giving a test on a half day.

Other Ideas for Half Days

You might also consider doing something very entertaining on a half day or perhaps, making that part of your class creed. While it should be academically motivated, the idea of doing something "fun" may be just enough to prod students into showing up.

For example, if you've studied the Victorian era, you might have a Mad Tea Party, complete with watercress sandwiches and Earl Grey Tea. If you're working on physics, one of these half days might be the great "Watermelon or Pumpkin Drop" from the roof of the gym. (Just some thoughts to consider!) And maybe, just maybe, this mild straying will give *you* a little boost too.

Just a final note from me: it's important for teachers to think about what their grading means to the kids, and being clear in what we want from students is imperative.

This year, I had my tenth graders answer a prompt in an essay format. When I began grading the essays, I had no idea what I was looking for. It was then that I figured out that I needed a rubric, and maybe the students would have done

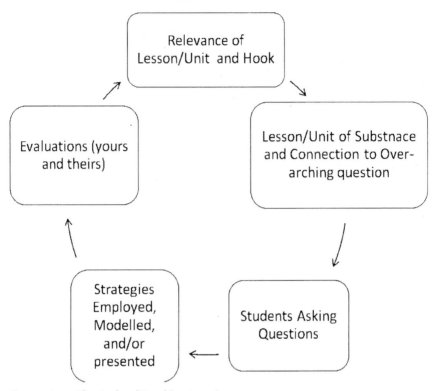

Figure 14.2.   The Cycle of Teaching Learning

better had I used a better approach to grading. For future reference, I found
many online programs that assist in the creation of rubrics! ~ Stacey

Hopefully, this chapter provided you with some ideas and strategies for
grading. This very necessary part of our jobs doesn't have to frustrate or bore
us. Rather, it can serve *our* agendas for the class as we move through our
cycle for each lesson and unit.

With all of these strategies employed within the first quarter of school,
you'll find that you are in very good shape for the second nine weeks. You'll
have a flow in each class.

Chapter Fifteen

Final Approach and Landing

Tah-dah! You made it! It's the end of the year. You're moving into final exams, final projects, and the bittersweet taste of end-of-year administrative work. How you plan your descent and landing is yet another means of increasing your satisfaction with this career and enhancing next year's adventure.

ME FIRST!

Because *you* and your sanity are the priority for your summer break, your planning for the final days should reflect that priority. This is how to begin the end! At some point in April, you'll want to make notes on your planner to start scheduling your summer time. (If your spring break falls in March, all the better! Use that time for scheduling!) All too often, teachers wait until the summer to schedule their time and appointments, and then run into issues. *Prioritize* your summer planning for your maximum rest and relaxation by:

- Nothing Time
- Required/Recommended Classes
- Vacation/Trips
- Appointments

Nothing Time

This time, as noted in chapter 3, is crucial, and it should be your first priority for the summer. *Block off this time* in your planner purposefully, in pen—anything that will help you cement it.

Seminars, Classes, Certifications

After marking off your two weeks of "nothing time" in the planner, look into and schedule any required/recommended classes for the summer. Keep tabs on your certification expiration dates, and consider pulling your certification hours from your personnel office for review every year at this time. Write down in your planner that you've pulled your data—that way, when you review your planner, you'll have a reminder for next year's dates. Keeping track of where you are with these requirements will help you plan. Schedule those classes *after* your nothing time or, at the very least, outside of a span of nothing time.

If you find that a course just isn't offered at any other time but right after school gets out, then make sure you've taken the two weeks *after* that course off as your nothing time.

Vacation

Vacation time is a bit more flexible for scheduling, if you plan ahead. Pinpoint a vacation/travel time that falls *after* those two weeks of nothing and at least two weeks *before* the start of the school year. Taking a vacation the week before you begin pre-service days is vacation nullification.

Remember how tired you are after taking a trip, especially with children? You need those two weeks to recuperate—your vacation from your vacation! Additionally, by planning in advance around March or April, your spouse or travel partner will have a much greater chance of synchronizing dates.

Also consider that the farther you're going to travel, the further back you want to plan. Overseas trips should be planned six months in advance or more (think winter break). Out-of-state trips work best if planned at least three months in advance (during spring break).

You're going to be spending oodles of time with flight arrangements and hotels, rental cars, etc. Taking those moments to do so well in advance will help you have a stress-free summer.

Appointments

After you've marked off your nothing time and your vacation, you then have the *available* dates for your annual checkups and exams. Prioritize in "double" as best you can. That is, schedule your dentist appointment and your children's dental appointments on the same day. Even one appointment seems to take over the day; thus, get it out of the way in one swoop. Calling months, as opposed to days, ahead of time increases the chance that you'll get that double.

Advice: If available, select morning appointments. Then, your day won't feel completely lost.

Family Events

More than likely, you'll have a few birthdays, anniversaries, or other family events to include on your planner for the summer break. In planning, you have to determine what events hold priority. For example, if your family events are more important than your vacation, then adjust your vacation around them. Whatever works for you!

However, these categories have been purposefully aligned to cater to the individual. Taking care of yourself and your needs *first*, will help you avoid that sense of the summer just slipping by. It sounds selfish, and it is. However, everyone suffers when you are stressed, not just you. You'll want to feel refreshed, happy, and ready to begin your next school year.

Note: Of course, the out-of-ordinary and emergency situations will arise. However, because you will have planned exceptionally well, you'll have a much easier time dealing with them.

IN-COMMON FINAL EXAMS

Our district creates our in-common, required exams. We're still using exams from five years ago, even though our curriculum has changed . . . grr!
~ Anonymous teacher

After you take care of *your* planning in March or April, it's time to look at May, when you'll be deep in the throes of providing students with study sheets for their finals. Your school may have a district or school-wide exam for your subject. A strategy to consider for a study guide is to have students create their own exam and questions.

For example, if you know that one of the points covered is the concept of *volume*, have them use their previous tests and notes to create a final exam question on volume, either together or solo—their choice. Not only will this strategy ease your burden of lecturing and repeating, but the students will gain more from the one-on-one interaction that you will be able to provide as needed.

"It's too risky!" naysayers squeak. "What if they don't 'cover' everything?"

It's in that *covering* that we are dead on our feet. It's a euphemism for "teacher talking." Considering that if you're using an in-common exam, probably based on an in-common syllabus or scope/sequence, the likelihood that you've presented students with the necessary material is pretty good. Also, you'll be right there, guiding them through their study.

For a moment, though, let's consider the thinking behind this anxiety-driven response. From where do we derive this fearful thinking? The idea that, unless the teacher him/herself does the exam prep *for* the students, then the exam prep is null? The relentless, monotonous covering of things is ineffective for both teacher and student. It wears us out and doesn't do a thing for the student.

If we are to ensure that students become the critical thinkers and learners we want them to be, then this is an opportunity to hand them the reins. Granted, it's a bit scary, but visualize: the students are working, either together or alone, with notes and books and more notes scattered all over the place. Studying is messy!

However, the teacher is, at some points, sitting with the students, and at other times, talking with groups. He/she is available for the students to clarify, rectify, or edify.

> *I remember you sitting with us, sometimes never saying a word. You almost always had that smile on your face, though. It said, "I'm here. I care. Let's do this." ~ AnnMarie*

This is a scenario in which the teacher provides the students with a depth of confidence in themselves: "You have the resources and the answers. You've got this."

It's not our job to study *for* the students. It's our job to show them *how* to study. What strategies did you use when in college or high school that you could share before starting a prep class? Your empathy will speak in volumes towards your sincere desire for their success.

> *This is definitely a good time to share any personal stories about tests. I shared my experience of failing the math portion of the GRE twice.*
>
> *The third time, I listened to some really inspiring, blood-pumping music so that I felt good going into the test. I passed the third time. When I shared this with the kids, they really listened and connected with me because they had, at some point, failed tests as well. It humanized me, even though it was the end of the year. ~ Stacey*

DIVORCING YOUR TRIED AND TRUE MULTIPLE-CHOICE FINALS

For those schools who allow teachers to create their own final exams, it's time to go to couples counseling. Some educators are married to their final exams. The beauty of a 150-question multiple-guess test is nothing short of glorious. It's tidy and neat. The idea of using anything else is adulterous. (Mind you, some of those exams are so old that they were created on a ditto machine in that yucky, smelly ink.)

After all, you took the time to create the test (or at least took the time to "steal" it). Also, using Scantrons saves you a bunch of precious minutes. "Plus, students do better on multiple-choice tests, don't they?" you might cautiously venture.

Then it must be that you are unselfishly giving them a better chance at getting a "good" grade for their final. With arms crossed, you utter your final, victorious harrumph. For the sake of the children, get a *divorce*.

There is a huge part of me that loves multiple-choice tests, but a much larger part that hates it. I've always thought that "short answer" or "essay"-style questions worked better for me as a student. With multiple-choice questions, I often second-guessed myself. With essay and short answer I was able to talk out the idea and get all my thoughts on paper to show the teacher what I knew.
~ Christina

Remember that nifty, overarching question you presented on your syllabus? If the goal of the year is to answer that question, then that question *is* your final exam. One question. Open book, open notes. Rubric for expectations.

Figure 15.1 is an example of how the final exam for our English II class might look. As long as this question has been revisited throughout the semester or year, students will have a strong measure of confidence in taking it.

Does this sort of exam take more time to grade? Yes and no. You are looking for fluency of thinking on these exams before any levels of correctness. How critically are your students thinking? How *well* are they synthesizing and applying the information, texts, sources, examples from their coursework?

You can determine the depth of a student's thinking more quickly than you realize, if that's what you're looking for. Additionally, because you're using an open test, cheating is less of an issue. (Yes, there are always ways, but by and large, the students simply can't do so without it being glaringly obvious.) Thus, you can grade another class's exams during this exam without having to be the test police, walking up and down.

Possibly, some may argue that such an exam doesn't accurately reflect what the student has learned. That depends on the depth of the question and the level of expectation. However, if the teacher creates a viable rubric that stresses concepts and knowledge, then this approach most certainly reflects the student's learning. If we want students to be critical thinkers, then our coursework and our exams must provide students with an opportunity to actually do it.

Based on what we've read, studied, and discussed in class, what <u>really</u> seems to drive our choices? Why do we do the things we do, whether good or bad?

You are expected to use your texts and notes for this exam and integrate information from them to support your ideas.

Figure 15.1.   Sample Final Exam Question

Also, teachers should consider how they're grading that final exam. They may experience less stress if they holistically grade. The student isn't going to use any corrections you make anyway because the class is over, so why mark and change every error? ~ AnnMarie

(*Note:* The best time to give students the final evaluation handout is right after the test!)

Just curious as to why the best time for final evals is right after a test? Because it's something for the students who are done early to do? In college, I hated doing final evals after a test for some reason. ~ Tori

Given that many students don't return after the exam, even though we still have instructional days, you'll receive the *most* feedback after the exams because students are required to take them. The more data you gather, the more authentic the image of what you've done with the class will be.

CATEGORICAL HOOPS

These are inevitable but necessary items on our last-days agendas. Whether this is the return of "checked-out" machines or textbook inventory, know that your final days are a mash-up of, well, everything. Prioritizing your tasks into categories will help you jump through these hoops with minimal stress.

Priority One: Grades

Grades, and the entering of the same, are your main priority. If you've held true to your vow of turnaround time and graded smartly, you should be in good shape. Of course, you're going to have some late work turned in by students. These late, generally incomplete/lackluster assignments *should be graded with as much effort as the students gave them*—quick, decisive grades will save your sanity. Don't ponder over trivialities when the student has more than likely thrown something together for the sake of points.

Priority Two: Final Conversations

At some point on these last days, you'll want to have a sit-down with the remaining students in the class. If you provided them with the final evaluation handouts already, then you can ask a few pointed questions and get more info, based on those evals. For example, you might say: "Based on the evals, I noticed that everybody pretty much hated the ___ project. Tell me more about that."

Another solid strategy is to hand out the class syllabus, again. This will help students "remember" what the class actually did. As you listen, take notes on the syllabus. By the time you're done, you'll have a list of what worked, what didn't, and why—a valuable resource for planning next year!

> *I remember sitting down as a class at the end of the year (after the exams) with the syllabus in front of us. I remember writing all over it and talking about what we liked and didn't like. I really enjoyed helping you be a better teacher for next year's students. I felt like I was helping them out! ~ Stacey*

Priority Three: Books

If only because this component of end-of-year tasks is so time-consuming and—let's face it—about as interesting as unsalted crackers, your next priority should be dealing with the textbooks. You'll have those few lingerers-on in your class who may volunteer to help. However, if they don't, try not to look too pitiful as you carry twenty, biggie-size-me, jumbo-large textbooks to and fro.

Priority Four: Paperwork

Whatever paperwork, forms, or office-type things need to be done, they should fall at the *end* of your priority list. Generally, this approach works well because administrators don't expect to receive this paperwork until the last days, which are (usually) teacher in-service days. Put them in a reachable, non-losable spot on your desk.

Priority Five: Cleaning and Straightening

Our surroundings impact our mindset, so to provide yourself with a positive sense of closure, leave your classroom clean and organized. This includes the mother of all organization issues: your desk.

Hopefully, because of your awesome turnaround time, you've managed to keep the paperwork flow under control for the most part. Thus, your desk organization should be relegated to throwing away old candy and coffee-stained memos. As you move through your grading and find those errant office supplies, make sure to put them in their appropriate place (or in that catch-all drawer, at least). The goal is to get stuff off of the desk.

Priority Six: Organization

Organizing files is no fun, and if you're lucky, you've got a very helpful student volunteer to file stuff. If you don't, then keeping your files in order is a helpful exercise. Again, hopefully, you haven't saved this task for the end of the year in a convergence of paper-clipped, rubber-banded, and crisscrossed papers. Otherwise, you're going to be there for a while. You don't want to leave this undone if at all possible.

I once volunteered with a teacher, helping her file and organize. Slowly, we worked out a system of individual student boxes and inflow/outflow. However, had we not done that, she would have been in big trouble. At the very least, organize at the end of the year! ~ AnnMarie

By the time you leave your classroom, your desk, file cabinets, and bookshelves should be straightened. If you prioritize by category, you can do it!

Make sure you know what your school's policies are on end-of-the-year stuff. Also ask: will you be switching classrooms? Will your classroom be used during the summer for any reason? Lock it up and take home what you treasure! ~ Stacey

THE STRATEGY WORKS

It's important that you understand the above points are not *sequential steps*. They are *prioritized chunks*. For example, don't expect to finish inputting all of your grades before starting on textbooks. Keep these categories as conceptual priorities. If you are up-to-date on grades in period three, then start a conversation with the class. If you're up-to-date on grades, have had your conversation, and you are current on textbooks in period five, dive into paperwork. It's a mental checklist: grades, conversation, textbooks, paperwork, cleaning, organizing.

You'll start the whole prioritization process over again on the next day: grades, conversation, books, paperwork, cleaning, organizing. As much as possible, include the students in the work. If you've created a sense of "us" or "the class," it will be evident here. Students who take responsibility for the physical class are more in tune with the abstract concept of the class.

As you walk out that door for the last time, smile. You've done your best. It's time to rest your body and mind. It's time to do *nothing*.

Chapter Sixteen

Teacher Triage and Final Thoughts

The entire approach of transparent teaching works best if you can begin before the school year starts. However, some of you may pick this book up in September or March, and I don't want you to get frustrated thinking that you can't incorporate any of these ideas into your classrooms immediately. You can!

Here's a prioritized outline form of what we've discussed, in the event you're starting in the middle of things. No matter where you are in the school year, you can accomplish these steps.

IN CLASS

- Learn students' names to the extent that you do not need to call attendance.
- Create a comprehensive teacher evaluation to determine what you may need to work on that includes as many components from this text as possible. (For example: teacher voice, grading, management, etc.)
- Have a class discussion about that evaluation and the class as a whole.
- Renew your commitment to the class and encourage them to do the same.
- Determine revised student and teacher expectations.
- Revamp rules as necessary.
- Teach students how to question.
- Start using "Ask Me a Question" strategy.
- Encourage student evaluation.
- Videotape or record yourself.

ON YOUR OWN

- Print out student contact information and create a log.
- Call every student's home.
- Emotionally prepare yourself for evaluation.
- Create or revamp a course outline for the remainder of the year.
- Start grading smarter.
- Begin weekly grade updates in class.
- Begin weekly parent e-mails.
- Critically evaluate your videotape or ask a friend to do so.
- As you drive home or to school, visualize your ideal class.

Ultimately, your goal is to create a sense of starting over. Believe it or not, students might embrace the concept. You may want to write out a heartfelt letter and read it aloud before you hand out your comprehensive teacher evaluation.

If you're artistic, consider introducing the legend of the Phoenix in some way, being reborn from the ashes. Use music, poetry, art, dance, a video with index cards, whatever will ensure a full stop of where you are to where you should be. By doing so, you'll reinforce and model this life lesson: "Never fear starting over."

In one of our classes, we did begin anew, at some point in September. Things were just not going well, so I felt we needed to regroup. I wrote a letter to the students that expressed my thoughts and feelings and read it aloud. We had a discussion, and then things got better.

I admit that first I felt some trepidation. The class was to change after all, and a change can be for better or worse.

However, what the sudden change did do was catch my attention. Since I was made aware of the change, I had to consider where the class was going, so I was receptive to the changes. This is a natural response for any individual placed in similar circumstances. Therefore, it's reasonable to conclude that, as long as the changes are worthy, there's nothing wrong in implementing them at any time throughout the year. However, in keeping with transparency, the student should be made aware of the impending alteration. ~ Daniel

Keep on in your transparency. See *people*, not just students. Laugh. Be humble. Model maturity. Freely communicate. Be concerned and consistent. Be calm and patient. Forgive. Care.

Think.

Learn.

Bibliography

Baumrind, Diana. "Effects of Authoritative Parental Control on Child Behavior." *Child Development* 37 no. 4 (1966): 887–907.

Bloom, Benjamin, M. D. Engelhart, E. J. Furst, W. H. Hill, and D. R. Krathwohl. *Taxonomy of Educational Objectives: The Classification of Educational Goals; Handbook I: Cognitive Domain.* New York: Longmans, Green, 1956.

Fay, Jim, and David Funk. *Teaching with Love and Logic.* Golden, CO: Love & Logic Press, 1995.

Wong, Harry, and Rosemary Wong. *The First Days of School: How to Be an Effective Teacher.* 4th ed. Mountain View, CA: Harry K. Wong Publications, 2009.

Index

About the Authors

Mindy Keller received her Bachelor of Arts degree in English from Florida Atlantic University in 1997, graduating *summa cum laude,* and began teaching in 1998. Her career spans from teaching remedial to advanced courses in English, as well as required and elective courses in theatre and debate, within both traditional and virtual environments. She has spoken at several conferences, including the College Board's AP Annual Conference of 2007, in Las Vegas. Her presentation focused on the use of Socratic questioning in the classroom as a means to enhance writing and critical-thinking skills. She is also a National Board Certified Teacher in English Language Arts—Adolescent/Young Adult.

Stacey Bruton earned her bachelor's degree in Secondary English Education from the University of South Florida in 2009. She has taught both middle school and high school, and currently, she works as an intensive-reading teacher at a Title I high school in Tampa, Florida. She enjoys spending time with family, friends, her two cats, and taking trips to Disney World in her spare time.

AnnMarie Dearman earned a Bachelor of Arts degree in English from Florida Atlantic University in 2007, graduating *summa cum laude*. She works as a home-school coordinator and as a tutor, where she enjoys the challenges of working with all grade levels in person and via the Internet. Aside from currently pursuing her M.Ed. in Curriculum and Instruction with Secondary English certification, AnnMarie also home schools her three spectacular children. The Dearman home base is currently in Port Saint Lucie, Florida.

Victoria Grant earned her bachelor's degree in Psychology from the University of Central Florida in 2004. After several years working as a second-grade teacher, she is now a stay-at-home mom to the sweetest one-year-old boy. Her husband currently serves in the U.S. Air Force, and she is a Key Spouse for his unit. She is also the Hospitality Coordinator for the VAFB Mothers of Preschoolers Group. In her spare time, she enjoys sewing, reading, and spending time with her friends and family.

Crystal Jovae Mazur is a costume and jewelry designer, residing in Chicago. She attended Florida State University, earning a Bachelor of Arts degree in Theatre Studies. While there, she continued to perform and write, but found her passion in costume design, studying all applications of design and construction. After graduation, Crystal moved to Chicago and worked as an apprentice in the costume shop at Steppenwolf Theatre. She continued with Steppenwolf as the Outside Project Coordinator, collaborating with companies and artists around the world. Currently, she is the resident Assistant Costume Designer for The Goodman Theatre. She has settled into a wonderful city life with her partner, Justin, and their three dogs—Bella, Freya, and Hemmie.

Daniel Powell graduated from Westwood High School in 2000. During his time in high school, he accumulated awards in science, art, writing, and theatre. He was a student of Ms. Keller during his junior and senior years. Since then, Daniel has attended Indian River State College, where he has furthered his education in the areas of English and history, and has devoted himself to pursuing his talents in writing as a career. Daniel lives in Fort Pierce, Florida, with his wife, Melissa, and his older brother, Robert. He illustrates and writes for zerolevel.com, and he is both author and artist for the webcomic, *Gunman*.

Christina Salvatore earned her bachelor's degree in English with a focus in Creative Writing and a minor in Journalism from Florida State University in 2007. After graduating, she obtained a job as a regional office manager for an insurance agency in Tallahassee, Florida. Christina is currently pursuing several freelance writing and editing positions to expand her portfolio. She currently resides in Tallahassee, Florida, with her fiancé, Andy, and their two dogs, Miguel and Hartlee.